CORPORATE ACCOUNTABILITY

Executive Policy and Leadership Series

HOWARD W. JOHNSON, *Editor*

■

CORPORATE

ACCOUNTABILITY

For What and To Whom

Must the Manager Answer?

PAUL O. GADDIS

HARPER & ROW, PUBLISHERS

NEW YORK, EVANSTON, AND LONDON

*To Alfred P. Sloan, Jr., whose
genius and generosity have benefited
the economic institutions of our
society in dimensions so broad that
only history will fully realize them.*

Contents

PART IV

Preface

The trouble with most books about management is twofold: First, practicing managers do not read them; and second, practicing managers do not write them. These two aspects of trouble are significantly related. Frederick Kappel remarked candidly in a recent publication that in his career he had found little in management literature to help him be a better manager.

Modern corporate managers are too busy practicing to find time to read and write in the discipline of their emerging profession. Apparently only the senior executive nearing retirement has made the effort to assert management concepts in writing, and fortunately there have been several important manager-written books contributed to postwar literature by senior management citizens. The scene in general, however, is reminiscent of the emerging medical profession in the decade before 1910, when medical academicians in schools did all the writing and most of the reading. Practicing physicians had time only to "cut and prescribe" and had little time to reflect about what they were doing and for what purpose.

As a member in the institution of corporate management, in mid-career and bolstered by some recent exposure to management thinking in the schools, I have attempted here to write a book on a subject of crucial importance to society and to managers in the Western world during the 1960s. The theme is corporate accountability as it is exercised by men who are managers. Accountability has been defined as *responsibility for causing something to happen*. This book is in essence an examination of the nature of this kind of responsibility, past and present, as it is borne by managers, and a consideration of how it may be discharged in the future. The writing has been motivated by my conviction that the business manager of today must achieve in some measure an understanding of his accountability if he is to preserve his identity and retain his mission within the society he serves.

A study of accountability in the corporate sector must begin with the institutions around which the business structure has been built. The first of these is the corporate form of organization, an association of human beings stemming from centuries of law and dogma. The second is the modern institution of men who are managers of industrial effort. The third is the institution of the professional calling as it has flourished in Western culture. The trail of investigation also leads into the relationship of the business world to the public institutions of our society, to government, labor, the academic world, and to those who are opinion formers.

In the writing I have made limited excursions into the fields of finance, law, economics, philosophy, and the social sciences, all of which border the structure of corporate accountability. These fields cover a broad spectrum, but only so broad as the arena in which industrial managers operate in their daily lives. Although I do not claim expertness in each component of this spectrum, I shall attempt to analyze the whole structure of accountability from the viewpoint of the manager who must respond to its demands.

This study grows out of a unique opportunity that was presented to me several years ago as an industrial manager with a large United States corporation. It was my good fortune to receive an appointment as a Sloan Fellow, involving a year of graduate study at the School of Industrial Management at the Massachusetts Institute of Technology. The privilege of participating in this study of industrial management came through the generosity of the Westinghouse Electric Corporation and the Alfred P. Sloan Foundation.

During the year at Cambridge, it was possible to discuss the topics of this book with the faculty and consultants at the M.I.T. and Harvard graduate management schools and to have access to the business libraries at these two institutions. Under the auspices of the Sloan program, I was also given access to the front offices of American corporations, where corporate accountabilty is currently a matter of serious concern. The analysis included a series of discussions with the chief executive officers of major industrial corporations and financial institutions. Other sessions were held with management consultants, officers of the New York Stock Exchange, and members of the United States Congress.

The investigation confirmed that senior business leaders do not at present share a common consensus regarding corporate accountability. However, each of those interviewed spoke positively and articulately about his own and his company's views, reflecting the results of deep consideration of the matter.

I want to record my gratitude for the continuous help, over a span of several years, from Douglas McGregor, professor of industrial management at M.I.T., and from Elting Morison, professor of industrial history at M.I.T. Without the stimulus of periodic discussions with these men, this effort could not have been carried through. Howard Johnson, dean of the school of industrial management at M.I.T., has upon several occasions offered me the benefit of his considerable experience, and his counsel and encouragement have been important. Dean Courtney Brown of the Columbia School of Business Administration has discussed with me his views concerning the key topics of this book and has expressed knowledgeable and valuable opinions.

I am also deeply indebted to the many leaders of industry who were willing to engage in serious discussion about corporate accountability. Among these, I owe a particular debt to Thomas J. Watson, Jr., business statesman and eminently successful businessman, for the insights provided by discussions with him. The progress of the work was materially assisted by the opportunity to review my concepts of accountability with Marshall K. Evans and Robert L. Wells of Westinghouse, whose depth of understanding of the topic was notable. The opinions and concepts expressed herein are my own, however, and can in no way be blamed upon any of those who were willing to help.

The subject matter of the book is divided into four parts. In Part I an earlier and great mode of business accountability is reviewed. This was the concept stemming from classical economics and laissez faire as they developed in the nineteenth century. It is an essential point of departure in proceeding to consider modern corporate responsibility. Part I also reviews the decay of the business Ethic, forecasting the change of the earlier accountability. An antithetical structure of accountability, called the twentieth-century model, is outlined in Chapter 4 as it has evolved in response to social forces. The new accountability has never been fully understood nor has it been accepted by either managers or the public. Many observers have concluded that Western industry has been unable to reconcile this new model with the important residuals of nineteenth-century accountability. Although this conclusion may be routine, its import is significant. Modern man cannot live without an economic creed.

The manifestations of this unresolved conflict are discussed

in Part II, in which the present status of corporate accountability is analyzed. Critics have alleged a lack of responsibility, and their charge is examined. In Part III, the unique role
of the professional calling in Western culture is considered.
The relationship between the professional role and the present institution of management is established, and the fea-
sibility of a management profession is weighed.

In the last section of the book, it is necessary to enter the
sensitive domain of "what should be." Part IV is offered as
an outline of solutions to the present problems of corporate
accountability. The emphasis is upon the *concepts* that will
provide a real institutional accountability for management—
a responsibility that is institutionally imposed and maintained
by management upon itself.

The concepts set forth in this book are addressed primarily
to the practitioners of industrial management, with the ex-
pectation that today's managers will redefine a clear structure of accountability in the years immediately ahead.

Cambridge, Massachusetts   PAUL O. GADDIS
January 1964

PART I

Great then is the good fortune of a state
in which the citizens have a moderate and
sufficient property.

—ARISTOTLE
  The Politics

1 An Introduction

The American economic republic has in hand . . . human and material resources, productive organization, and political, financial, and economic instruments capable of dealing justly and generously with all foreseeable social demands and situations. It merely needs political, economic, and business brains and imagination to use them.—ADOLF A. BERLE in *The American Economic Republic*, 1963

Responsible business leaders cannot live without an economic creed that tells them to whom they are accountable and for what.

In the recent past, businessmen had their creed, built upon the classical economics of Adam Smith and his disciples. In the great years of this creed, owners and proprietors in business found a clear responsibility. Their own actions were guided unerringly, or so they believed, toward the public good and their own gain. In turn, the men who worked for them knew how and why the employee was accountable to ownership.

In the present years, responsibility based upon ownership has lost its sparkling clarity. As a result of the widely dispersed holdings of voting stock in large corporate organizations, ownership has become an entity that often must be interpreted with the aid of a lawyer. The remnants of understanding of the business creed of classical economics are disappearing fast, and despite a great deal of theorizing, no one has yet come forward with a new concept that will give the manager any real understanding of his accountability.

This leaves modern corporate enterprise, and the men who run it, in a vulnerable position. For more than ten years, observers of this enterprise have been charging that our corporations are no longer effectively accountable for their actions, not only because of ownership diffusion but also because the virtues of regulation by market forces have been lost. These observers say flatly that no appropriate substitute for the former accountability has been established. Their charges have not been answered.

Present-day managers do not agree with the details of these charges, as we shall see, but they know in their hearts that the erosion of accountability is a fact. They also know that when men had a clear business creed and followed it, business performance was keen and effective. Moreover, in those bygone years when the purposes of business were clearly related to the objectives of the society, the long-term survival of free enterprise was assured.

These two purposes—efficient performance within business and the effective survival of enterprise in the society—are the central concern of contemporary business managers. If managers are going to serve these purposes and answer the critics who assert that there is no present corporate accountability, they need to come to grips with these questions:

What is business accountability, and how did it come to be?

What is its real status now?

What must managers do, individually and collectively, to improve accountability?

If a man is accountable, he is by definition "liable to be called to answer in judgment." An agent is accountable when he must answer for the use of resources with which he has been entrusted, and when he is responsible for causing results that are generally understood to be desirable.

The framers of the Constitution established an American tradition when they declared that a holder of power within a sphere of influence must answer for that power in "another place." According to this tradition, managers who have been granted power and privilege within the corporation must be answerable for them in some manner to another place outside the corporation. *Accountability* is the vital thread between the corporate environment and the "other" place. When this accountability is viable, clear, practiced, and accepted, the producing organisms in industry are attuned to their society; industrial achievement and growth can be remarkable; the channels through which managers may contribute to the society are opened; and the opinion formers can be counted upon to defend and further the interests of producing industry, at least part of the time. All these conditions prevailed when the late and frequently lamented nineteenth-century form of business accountability was at its peak.

The Anglo-Saxon urge to constrain men in power by checks and balances is countered by another basic strain in the American character. The American is deeply rooted in the Judaeo-Christian culture, which leads him to believe that there is an ultimate meaning in the circumstances of his life and that thereby both he and his nation are dedicated to a special mission. He inherits the conviction that the pursuit of gain is not an end in itself but must be justified by the use to which the gain is put. Thus his work on earth is a calling, attuned to the larger values of his society, and if he heeds its rigorous demands, he need not be accountable to any other place on earth. In the words of the 1958 Rockefeller Brothers Fund Report, "This strain of self-imposed accountability has been a persistent note of our society."

Significantly, men who work self-accountably seem to work more effectively.

Americans are thereby caught between the demands of two polar schools of thought. They face the appeal of dynamic, creative self-responsibility on the one hand, supporting *human productivity* in its broadest meaning, and the pull of form and regulation on the other, protecting *social righteousness*. By selection of a middle course—a synthesis—both mainstream principles can be heeded, and this blending within the economic sphere is management's current challenge.

What is needed is a business accountability, that is, a system for answerability to the society, which must be double-barreled in its purpose. First, it should preserve the dynamics and the creativity of responsible leaders; second, it should make our business enterprise responsive to the objectives, both economic and social, of the society as a whole.

Such an accountability can be designed and built in the modern scene only by the institution of management, by the concerted efforts of managers themselves acting where other would-be architects have failed.

2 Origins

> The great and chief end, therefore, of men's uniting into commonwealths, and putting themselves under government, is the preservation of their property.—JOHN LOCKE, *Essay on Civil Government*, 1690

Today's manager suffers from an uneasy regard for the future of enterprise under the system in which he practices, no matter how successful his efforts may be in the present. He is concerned that he is drifting apart from his world—that the gulf of misunderstanding which separates him from his contemporaries in government, labor, and intellectual circles is growing steadily larger. An implicit part of his reaction is his yearning for the time, not so many years ago, when there was a rationale that explained the purposes of business and industry to all. This rationale, stemming from the concepts of classical economics, precisely related his purposes to the objectives of the whole society in which he lived.

His favorite subject of nostalgia is the structure of business accountability founded upon ownership, which is termed the nineteenth-century model in this discussion. In this chapter, the several precedents of the nineteenth-century accountability will be traced. The object is not to develop the history of enterprise in these years before 1800, but to identify those factors that led to the magnificently un-

7

clouded nineteenth-century understanding of businessmen's responsibility.

The age of feudalism was an age in which there was no separation between a man's practical life—his work—and his whole political, religious, and social life. His home life and his occupational life were inextricably bound together at the same site. The church and the state were all-pervading and commingled, and there was no economic sphere in any way apart from them.

The picture of feudalism is often that of the manor—an autocratic form of society founded upon ownership which was the source of legitimacy for all power. This was a concentrated, stultified kind of ownership, a prerogative limited to an extreme few—the lords of the manor. The privileges of ownership, where it existed, were virtually unlimited and were proscribed only by the vagaries of the "natural law," which was above the lords. In this overly simplified picture, there was the strong element of fealty, that is, the personal fidelity of the vassal to his lord, in return for which the vassal enjoyed a form of security.

The preindustrial Western society was not a society that sanctioned the idea of personal gain or acquisitiveness. One of the constant dictums of the church in the Middle Ages was, "No Christian ought to be a merchant." To be sure, avarice and greed were part of human nature, then as now, and the medieval lords in their acquisitive ventures knew when to turn their backs on the teachings of the church. Nevertheless a large-scale system based upon the recognized concept of personal gain by each participant was unthinkable. Only those inclined to blasphemy would have spoken of a "profit motive."

Since society in that era did not sanction personal gain, it could not have general markets for commodities or services. There were periodic individual markets, at the fairs and in the towns, but there was no market system. Trading was minimal, unorganized, and inaccurately recorded.

The elements of land, labor, and capital did not exist as the abstractions that economists now use. Consider the case of land in England, where the vast bulk of the people have always been tenants. In the decade before 1700, there were only about 175,000 landowners out of a population of five million, or 3.5 per cent. This small group came into possession of their land mostly through inheritance, as a result of judicious family ventures in the past. No member of the landed gentry would conceivably treat his land as a transferable commodity, but rather regarded it as an inherited right.

Similarly, there was no labor market. There were serfs, but these were bound to the manor by duty; there were apprentices who served their masters, but wage rates and hours of both master and apprentice were set by a guild.

Those who controlled funds in the precapitalist era were all staunchly committed to the status quo. The concepts of *change* and *risk* were quite foreign to them. Although there were funds in these centuries, there was no risk capital and there were no capitalists. *Innovation*, as an accepted and rational factor in the society, was not only lacking, but also was viewed as a cardinal sin by the church and state, by the aristocracy, and by the guilds. Other unknown factors were the trained official, who existed only in embryo, and the manager, whose function was not yet conceived.

This was a stable, relatively comfortable, traditional world, under command of the fortunate few. It was self-satisfied and self-reproducing through many generations. It was preoccupied with forming, studying, and exerting a strict accountability, chiefly in the religious and political dimensions, upon its populace, even to a considerable extent upon the lords of the manors who sat atop the pyramids of authority. At all levels, it was a society that would not yield easily to change.

Foundations for Capitalism

> Revolutions begin in the best heads, and run steadily down to the populace.—PRINCE VON METTERNICH

The birth agony of the market system began in the thirteenth century and continued into the nineteenth. In its final impacts, this long process was to destroy completely the feudal structure of accountability. The most dramatic change during these years was the Industrial Revolution in the second half of the eighteenth century. It was manifested in three abrupt alterations in the conduct of human lives: an agricultural revolution, a communications revolution, and the manufacturing revolution.

This dramatic revolution was preceded by profound changes in human thinking, which are of particular importance to the subject of this book. First, there was the rise of scientific curiosity and technological exploration. Sophisticated accounting and bookkeeping were imported into Europe and Britain from Venice. The innovator and the experimenter were tolerated for the first time, thus setting the stage for the age of Newton and his creative contemporaries and for the later development of the specialist and the trained official.

But the most important prerequisite to the development of the later concept of ownership was a sanction of the role of personal gain. A code of economic conduct based upon this role would have to be achieved in the face of a broadly accepted scheme of social ethics and against the rigorous provisions of church law and secular law. As early as 1700 this established scheme of ethics began to give way. A picture of "economic man," who followed the trail to gain wherever it led him, began to emerge. By 1800 the concept of personal gain was not only securely established but was also well explained and rationalized.

There is still much controversy in scholarly circles regarding the reason for this basic change in outlook. One school of thought, inhabited by those scholars who tend to trust impersonal forces, believes that this revolution in thinking was sparked by irresistible changes in the economic environment—the influx of wealth from overseas commerce, expanding markets and population, and technological improvements. Other scholars, led by Max Weber,[1]* believe that the change had its source in human, religious motivation, and specifically in the Reformation of the sixteenth century. Capitalism was the social counterpart of Calvinist theology.

For present purposes, this new ethic may be regarded as an ingredient in the new thinking, whether or not it was causative. It has been dubbed the "Protestant Ethic," although it is now recognized that it was part of a general intellectual movement participated in also by Catholic philosophers and had many roots in the whole stream of Judaeo-Christian culture. It is examined here because of the distinct influence it still exerts in some aspects of corporate accountability.

The core of the Ethic was the idea of a "calling," which was no longer the state of life to which a man was predestined by Heaven, but a responsible and demanding enterprise that he could select himself. To labor fruitfully in this calling was then a spiritual end in itself, not merely an economic means. The calling dictated a rational conduct—a self-denying emphasis upon hard work, diligence, thrift, sobriety, and prudence.

A primary tenet of the Reformation was that man's chief

* Superscript numbers refer to Notes at end of text.

concern on earth was the glory and sovereignty of God, and that in serving this cause far above himself, man also served his own well-being on earth. This was a reaffirmation of the basic strain in the Judaeo-Christian culture, which has always required that men must serve a purpose removed from and superior to their immediate interests. Life was dedicated to reward in the hereafter and also in the here-and-now on earth. Reward came via self-realization in hard work, which also resulted in accumulation of material wealth. The accumulation of wealth was wholly sanctioned, as long as it was used in accordance with the Ethic, for it was the result of demonstrated virtue. But the wealth always became *capital*, an almost sacrosanct material that one never used for mere consumption. This integral self-denial was an important regulator because it kept acquisitiveness within proper bounds and ensured that wealth was utilized appropriately.

Lord Russell's acid pen recalls his childhood in Victorian England, when the Ethic was at its peak:

When I was a child the atmosphere in the house was one of puritan piety and austerity. . . . Although there were eight servants, food was always of Spartan simplicity, and even what there was, if it was at all nice, was considered too good for children. . . . Cold baths all the year round were insisted upon, and I had to practice the piano from seven-thirty to eight every morning although the fires were not yet lit. My grandmother never allowed herself to sit in an armchair until the evening. Alcohol and tobacco were viewed with disfavour although stern convention compelled them to serve a little wine to guests. Only virtue was prized, virtue at the expense of intellect, health, happiness, and every mundane good.[2]

Finally it should be noted that the Ethic placed great value on the independence of the individual. In its Protestant strain, it made the individual rigorously accountable, without need of human intermediary, to his God. The conscientious puritan continually supervised his own state of grace.

Validation of Ownership

> What we accumulate by way of useless surplus does us no honor.—HENRY FORD

It was well for the new entrepreneur of the infant middle class to know what he was after and to understand why his ventures were virtuous. But it remained for someone else to explain how a system of many such "economic men" would work, and indeed whether it could work. Many analogies have been drawn that note the critical need for a business philosophy now, in the mid-twentieth century, similar to the need at the time of the Industrial Revolution.

The earlier need was supplied by the classical economists Adam Smith, Ricardo, Malthus, and John Stuart Mill. Dr. Smith founded the concept of natural liberty in the market sphere, and thereby gave legitimacy to the market system in the eyes of the public for generations to come. He created the idea of a sovereign consumer to whom all production was oriented.

If the market system was to work, three forces had to be assumed as continually at work within it. First, each producer and distributor in the system must at all times act in self-interest, that is, to bring the greatest return to himself. Second, there must be a *regulator* acting continuously upon this force of self-interest. The regulator was to be the competition within the market place; this competition had to meet certain specifications, and Smith started the singularly unfortunate custom among economists of trying to define a state of competition by a single adjective. In Smith's day, it was called "perfect" competition, and this term defined a sufficiently vigorous competition among many firms to constrain any single firm in the market from being able to influence its returns, or the wages it paid, contrary to the all-powerful influence of the system itself.

The third force that classical economists assumed was the continuous capacity of the consumer to exercise his sovereignty, to maximize his satisfactions through selective purchasing in a free market. If the consumer were to have this capacity, he needed both the will and the competency to exercise the "dollar vote" in the market.

A market system with these inputs could be counted upon for a set of outputs that at first glance may appear commonplace but which on further scrutiny are truly remarkable—perhaps as remarkable as any system of dynamics that human vision has penetrated. First, the laws of the system impose a competitive price, or the best feasible price for consumers, on products and services sold within it. Prices will not stray, by human whim or design, away from a close relationship with the costs of production. Second, the wages that secure the needed services of labor must be competitive in the labor market; thus the wage rates are set by the market at the best feasible level for the worker and at a level that permits the employer to compete fairly with other employers. The producer who tries to buck this stern system with regard to prices or wages finds himself without customers or workers.

The third output of the system controls for each good or service the *quantity* of production to best meet the needs of the consuming public. By means of the dollar vote acting upon the price mechanism, which in turn influences the returns to producers, the changing and fickle wants of the consumer are readily fulfilled. One producing firm throttles its unwanted line of production while another increases its output to meet increasing demand.

Fourth, and of vital importance, the market system providentially regulates the assignment of the factors of production—the land, labor, and capital—which (after the Industrial Revolution) are transferable entities that can be used by the entrepreneur, and which are abstractions that can be grasped by the scholar of economics. The factors flow within the system to the frontiers of production where they are most needed for the good of the society.

The final regulative output from the system is the beneficial control of the *incomes* of all the human participants in production. Where returns to producers are too high, other potential producers rush in and set up shop, and their production serves to lower the returns. Workers migrate from one area or firm to another, with the result that unduly high or low wage levels will be eradicated.

These were the remarkable advantages to be accrued in the free market system. But there was something even more remarkable about it. It was assumed to operate infallibly without benefit of commissariats, bureaus, and other breeds of supervising organizations and without need for planners, directives, plans, mandates, regulations, etc. In short, it posed no need for omniscient human beings, who must sit at the fulcrums of power to direct the machinery.

From the point of view of accountability, the most important facet of the classical market system was its acceptance in the society of the time. The system complemented the Ethic, which powerfully governed the thinking of the economically aggressive citizens who were forging a middle class. Those who were seeking their self-fulfillment and reward through achievement in the here-and-now, and who were self-accountable to an Authority not on earth, were tailor-made citizens for the market society. These participants in the system knew what they wanted to do and how their role would affect the society in which they lived.

Aside from the participants, it was critically important that the learned observers also accept the market system. Natural liberty in the market place fitted the broader political philosophy of natural liberty then espoused by the intellectuals and the radicals. The demonstrations of Sir Isaac Newton in science and the reflections of John Locke in political philosophy together profoundly influenced the values and the thinking in England, on the Continent, and in America during the eighteenth century. Locke's positions, as set forth particularly in his second essay on government, written in 1690, are examined briefly here because of the importance of his work in relation to accountability.

In Locke's view, government had a limited function and existed solely to preserve the property of the individual. To him, "life, liberty, and estate" was a supreme concept. Locke had come under the strong influence of Newton, his contemporary, and the natural laws of Newtonian physics. He came to believe that the preservation of freedom and democratic process could best be achieved in a government of balanced powers, analogous to the balance, the action and reaction, in physics. He thereby became an early advocate of "countervailing powers," a form of pluralism in which the good of all automatically came out of the continuous resolution of conflicts among the power centers, each of which must be maintained by the society in a state of nourishment approximately equal to that of the others. The similarity of the dynamics in this political abstraction to those in the market system of classical economics is apparent.

Thus, as the nineteenth century began, three mature and mutually supportive forces—an Ethic, a market system, and a scheme of political philosophy—formed the bedrock for the subsequent development of a firm structure of business accountability. Many embellishments would be applied to all three as economic society prospered, but the essences would remain unchanged for about one hundred years.

But most importantly for the subject of this writing, at the dawn of the nineteenth century the concept of ownership had been sanctified. The factors of production were commodities that could be bought and sold—and owned. Personal property was a reward, if only as a by-product, in the Ethic; the striving for it was a requisite input for a functioning market system; and the prevailing philosophic opinion was oriented to the protection of it. Ownership would be the first bastion of accountability in the business world.

Corporate Form

> It [the corporation] is an arrangement by which hundreds of thousands of men who would in days gone by have set up in business for themselves put their money into a single huge accumulation and place the entire direction of its employment in the hands of men they have never seen, with whom they never confer.—WOODROW WILSON, in the Annual Address before the American Bar Association, Chattanooga, Tennessee, 1910

The great market scheme of Adam Smith and his disciples was a fairly close fit to the realities of economic life at the end of the eighteenth century. But even during the ten years that Smith devoted to writing the *Wealth of Nations*, forces were pushing this early and simple economic world toward increasing complexity. Each force weakened the integrity of the classical model of the market, and it is a tribute to the care of its construction that many elements of the model have survived a century and a half of complicating forces.

One of these complicating forces was quite vigorously alive, but very young, in 1766 when Smith started work in earnest on his monumental book. This was the tendency of small groups of individuals to organize themselves for various purposes into a "body" that would represent them all in pursuing their task. Since ancient times, the body had been called a "corporation," and was organized in accordance with the law's age-old habit of recognizing men and a "body politic" as two kinds of persons. The body had rights and duties of its own, which were not the same as the rights and duties of its members.

Adam Smith's concept of the market system did not encompass corporations acting in place of his "firms" (proprietorships and partnerships). He took little note of the infant status of corporations and gave them little or no future in the sphere of business. His reason was significant: He did not believe that corporations, which he regarded as impersonal organizations, could ever act with *sufficient self-interest* to participate actively and properly in the market and make the market work.

Yet in all Western civilizations, and before them, men have shown an irrepressible desire to associate, to incorporate.[3] Although the corporate form was known in Greece in the sixth century before Christ, it was under ancient Roman law that the corporation was firmly recognized as the basic response to the human need for collective endeavor. The law of Rome[4] clearly distinguished the identity of the members from that of the corporate whole; it gave to the latter identity the form and rights of a fictive person, possessing legal rights and (importantly) the right to *own*. Through the Middle Ages, these concepts were refined and, shortly after 1600, included the idea that this fictive person did not need to die, that is, it was "immortal." Also at this time, the damning thought that the corporate person was "soulless" and had no conscience made its first appearance.[5]

Although men had always sought the right to organize and collectively pursue their own ends, the state had always jealously guarded the privilege of enfranchising corporations. Centuries of canon law had yielded the concession theory, which held that the corporation could exist only as a creature of the state. That is, the state may under rigorously defined circumstances permit the birth of a corporation. There was also a train of thought that held the corporation to be inevitably, by its very existence, an enemy of the state. Thomas Hobbes, an articulate advocate of an absolutely sovereign state,[6] who has influenced strong men in politics for four centuries, likened the growth of corporations in the state to the growth of ascarides (worms) in "the entrails of a natural man." Thus it was early established that the private corporation was always potentially in conflict with an aggressive state. Hobbes was saying that the systems of human activity within the corporate microsphere could not be reconciled to the purposes of the macrosphere (the state), no matter what kind of structure of corporate accountability was applied.

In England and on the Continent in the eighteenth and nineteenth centuries,[7] the privilege of incorporation was jealously guarded and was used generally for the benefit of the crown or state. Several of the states of the American union were born as chartered corporations of the English crown. The early blendings of the business venture with the corporate form have become infamous as landmarks of public travail and private abuse because of spectacular corporate failures in France and in England (the notorious "South Sea Bubble") in the first quarter of the eighteenth century.[8]

For the next one hundred years after these failures, the business corporation remained a discredited device. It was thoroughly unaccepted and unforeseen in colonial America at the time when the great political architects of the new world were devising a government and a society that emphasized the sanctity of private property. In 1820, an early American text on economics advised that "every moneyed corporation is prima facie injurious to the national wealth." But the human urge to incorporate would not be stifled, and it was in fact stimulated by accelerating technological industrialization and the resultant need for more powerful business organizations. In England, the Act of 1862 was the "Magna Carta of cooperative enterprise" in that it placed the corporate form and "legal personality" within easy reach of reasonably qualified citizens. The state still "made" corporations, but it did so in the same way it made marriages by granting a license to persons who wanted to marry. The concession theory of corporate law was dying.

In the United States, the concept of the corporation was particularly irrepressible. Alexis de Tocqueville commented in 1840 that, "Americans of all ages, all conditions, and all dispositions, constantly form associations. They have not only commercial and manufacturing companies, in which all take part, but associations of a thousand other kinds,— religious, moral, serious, futile, extensive or restricted, enormous, or diminutive." Unselective and easy methods of legal incorporation began to contribute to the shady status of some segments of American business in the late nineteenth century, and resulted before long in an era of wholesale "charter mongering." Advertisements from western and southern states seeking incorporators flooded the east, stressing phrases like "Incorporation better than Partnership" and "No books need be kept for public inspection anywhere."[9]

After the turn of the century, vigorous prosecution of corporations under the Sherman Antitrust act was carried on in the Roosevelt, Taft, and Wilson administrations. But during these years, the corporation began to win respectability in the eyes of public opinion and to become accepted by the public as a justifiable and necessary instrument for production and distribution. As the corporation became accepted, it began to multiply copiously. In the American colonies before the War of Independence, there had been twenty-one business corporations, of which only one was a manufacturing business. In the United States in 1960, there were eleven million business firms of all types, of which over a million were corporations.

Thus has the corporation grown in stature, from an early avocational habit of men to a promotional device abused by governments and citizens, and finally in the twentieth century, to a wealth-generating organism that is the heart of the industrial structure of Western civilization. The United States corporate establishment owns a half-trillion dollars in assets, or one-third of the aggregate national wealth of the United States, and employs four of every nine Americans. The corporation has become the instrument of business accountability in the United States.

The architects of this modern corporation have created a business world that was not intended or foreseen by the classical economists, the seventeenth-century political philosophers, and the builders of the Ethic, and in so doing they have forever altered the concept of ownership. In the collectivization of corporate ownership by the means of diffused equity holdings, these architects have enormously increased the power of the corporation to perform its mission in the generation of wealth and in the prosecution of large-scale and orderly innovation. But out of this gain has also come loss because the new collective ownership of the corporation (while it has to some extent alleviated the old uneasy relationship between the corporation in the abstract and the public consensus) has become one more factor tending to compromise the substance of accountability. Management is only now beginning to assess the magnitude of the compromise.

3 Nineteenth-Century Model

> I am the good shepherd: the good shepherd giveth his life
> for the sheep. But he that is an hireling, and not the shep-
> herd, whose own the sheep are not, seeth the wolf coming,
> and leaveth the sheep, and fleeth: and the wolf catcheth
> them, and scattereth the sheep. The hireling fleeth, because
> he is an hireling, and careth not for the sheep.—JOHN, 10

Classical economics and the market system were widely
accepted throughout the Western world during the nineteenth century and up until about 1914. If the United States
was to build its business civilization, it was apparent early
that widespread acceptance and understanding of a market
ethic and system would be required here too. Yet no simple
transplanting of European economic ideas would suffice.
In the founding days, Jefferson, Hamilton, Paine, and all
their remarkable contemporaries had not merely transplanted
the stream of democratic political thinking from Aristotle to
John Locke—they had added unique American features.

The classical economists in the Old World were, for the
most part, scientists, and they worked toward the fundamental objective of science—to increase human understanding. But United States businessmen are activists, and their
fundamental aim is to influence action, that is, action in the
business sphere, and when necessary to provide a favorable
environment for business, in the national sphere.

Businessmen in general reject the concept of ideology because of several unfortunate connotations of the word. It brings to mind all the political excesses of the first half of the twentieth century: communism, fascism, and others. It also implies a visionary kind of theorizing. The word, however, is much simpler when used in its denotation of "the manner of thinking of an individual, group, or class." Where the ideology is well constructed and well propagated, it leads to dynamic action, which may be beneficial or harmful, depending upon the values and goals of those who constructed it. In America a very effective business ideology was constructed, which was essentially a blended adaptation of the classical market system, the Ethic that grew from the Reformation and the Judaeo-Christian traditions, and the democratic political point of view. Like all ideologies, this one used the devices of selectivity, simplification, and the symbol. It was selective because it omitted information that did not support it; it was simple because it pictured ideas in black or white rather than the "gray" descriptive language of science.

The elements of this American adaptation had profound effect upon early business accountability.[1] The primary element was respect for the productive achievements of capitalism and the market system in America. These achievements were tangible, hard to argue with, and steadily becoming more impressive throughout the nineteenth and into the twentieth centuries. The system was making a magnificent response to the needs of the consumers.

Outside the area of the market place, the American adaptation could point to three significant accomplishments. First, United States business had created within itself a spirit of service to the society, in which men could legitimately and constructively discharge their obligations to their fellow men. Second, the system had provided an opportunity for personal achievement in business, with resulting social recognition, to all those with the talents to use it. Third, and most important, the American system, with its basis in economic freedom, established for men their freedom in the political, religious, and personal spheres.

Here again it is important to note the reasons for these accomplishments, as they were explained in the American adaptation. Americans did not find the answer to their successes in abundance of natural resources, or in industrious ancestry, or in hard work, for all these factors had been present in other societies without comparable achievements. The basis of the ideology was that Americans at the beginning of the nineteenth century had found a new way to release human energy, a new basis for human relationships in the production of wealth. This new way comprised sturdy Yankee traits: puritanism, optimism, nationalism, individualism, the concept of the "calling," and the universalism that demanded equal opportunity for all.

From the standpoint of business accountability, there were two important features of this new way: its emphasis upon morally responsible, self-accountable individuals, and its strict regard for the individual's right to own and control property. The first was rooted in a strong concern for the freedom of the individual, and in the Protestant Ethic. The ideal society was one in which men of personal integrity could be granted wide freedom for positive action and could be trusted to act in accordance with a sober sense of moral accountability. This ideal would be applicable not only to the wealth-producing groups in the economy, but also to all groups in the society such as lawyers, politicians, scientists, educators, soldiers, and journalists. The firm right of the individual to hold and enjoy property came directly from the sanctification of ownership, previously discussed, and was in keeping with Jefferson's "nation of small landholders."

The American adaptation molded all preceding systems to fit the United States situation, and set the stage for the structure of corporate accountability, which allowed American business to flourish in the nineteenth century.

The flavor of this nineteenth-century accountability is boldly depicted in a small book called *Imagination in Business*,[2] written in 1909 by a merchandising executive in New York. This book, now long out of print, was one of the series of inside revelations on how to get ahead in business, which Americans have been writing since the days of Ben Franklin. It was written at the peak and near the end of the era of unadulterated nineteenth-century business philosophy. In his book (chap. V), the author described his experiments with one Mills, a young clerk whom he had tried unsuccessfully to make into a businessman. After several months of intense efforts, Mills had been unable to come up with a single good idea to increase the sales of his employer. Hence the author gave him this final, unsolicited advice, which is a capsule of the businessman's creed of that day:

Lie low, my boy. Keep out of prominence as much as you can, and go down on your knees tonight and thank God that you have got a situation where you are paid all that you are worth. I don't mean that you are a bit inferior to thousands of other young men who are in the stores and wholesale houses in this city; but you, like them, are simply sitting upon the head of the *one brainy man who sits in the counting-room. He* has to solve all these problems. You and fifty others in your establishment are just sitting on top of his head, like so many dead weights. If the business prospers you expect a raise of salary, when it is *his* headwork that has gained every inch of the progress. *He has to carry you all.**

The "man" to whom the author referred was the owner, who was also the manager and in control of the business. For all the reasons that have been cited earlier, the owner

* Italics added.

was the anchor who secured the enterprise and whatever power it wielded to acceptance and respectability in the society—in short, to legitimacy. In the elementary model of nineteenth-century accountability, the hireling, the salaried man (who was always one step removed from full respect in the business community), was fully accountable to the ownership for his performance of work. The employee knew, moreover, why he was so accountable. In the 1909 book, the young clerk Mills, even before receiving the final bitter advice, decided that he "wanted to stay where he was," that is, at a fixed and somewhat permanent salary level.

Even in an elementary model, it is at the top of the accountability pyramid that subtlety and complexity enter into the picture. The crux of the accountability problem is at this point. To whom, and in what manner, was the owner accountable? First, the owner had put on the mantle of moral responsibility, to be exercised as he saw fit. He and everyone knew that abuse was always potential in the system. He knew that acquisitiveness could slip over the delicate border into avarice, sloth, or laziness, or that an Epicurean bent could creep in to prevent an owner's effective action in his own self-interest, thereby sabotaging a crucial input to the market system. Therefore the owner, in continually "supervising his own state of grace," had a solemn if unwritten contract enjoining him to act responsibly in the terms of that day.

The owner also shared the great responsibility for preserving the integrity of the market system, with its classical self-regulating mechanism. This absolved him of any undue preoccupation with general responsibilities to society and freed him to devote all his energies to his primary tasks in the generation of wealth. The market system, if it were kept oiled, took care of many details for him: It set prices and quantities, regulated incomes, cared for the consumers' desires, and allocated the factors of production. In the American adaptation, it did more than this; it provided an adequate personal outlet for achievement, self-fulfillment, and prestige for those who were worthy.

And how did the whole society, including the employee, view all this? The employee understood, at least implicitly, the mode of accountability of his employer-owner, and he accepted it. After all, he was a participant in the same Ethic. The nineteenth-century liberal, even on the radical fringe, was under the influence of Locke and Newton and Smith. In England, this liberal was confronted with the ten-hour day worked by eight-year-old children in the mine pits of Northumberland; the fourteen-hour days at the textile factories; and the mill owners who used their mills as a harem. To all these cases, the liberal's response was some version of "laissez-faire" or "let them (the owners) alone," for he believed that natural liberty was working to build a new world and that order was forming beneath all the chaos. These liberals were not callous; they were concerned with human welfare, but like their brethren of all generations, they established their own criteria for welfare, and in that era, welfare was viewed in a mechanistic framework.

The use of the corporate form in business complicates the elementary model, but not so much that the threads of the nineteenth-century pattern cannot be clearly discerned. The long evolution of the law of association, when applied to business, had culminated in a corporate law that regarded the corporation primarily as an instrument of the owners. The law clothed this instrument with limited liability, the means for perpetuation (often termed *immortality*), and the effective means for concentrating private resources, all for the purpose of engaging in private enterprise. The interests of the owners were more important than any obligations to the state, even though the corporation owed its life to the state. The only substantial restrictions that this law placed on the entrepreneurial conduct of the corporations were those that protected either the owners' interests or the rights of others who contributed, that is, creditors, bondholders, supplier, and similar investors.

Thus the law reinforced the concept of ownership. But, then as now, business and the society were a great deal more complicated than the law portrayed them. The philosophy of the corporation leaders followed the tenets of classical economics and the American adaptation: He who pursued earnings advanced the welfare of the society. Also, these leaders were usually as committed to the Ethic as were their small-business associates. Hence, if the corporation was viewed as "a man writ large," as many of the early United States corporations were, then it could be endowed with human, personal characteristics. And it could be simply substituted for the proprietor in the elementary model of business accountability.

The corporation made provision for the separation of ownership from control and thereby gave a charter to the managerial function. However, in the early days of United States corporations, owners, managers, and directors were generally the same persons; in any case, the managers could identify the person or persons who represented ownership of their companies. The accountability of the manager to ownership was easily constructed and rigorously practiced.

As this accountability was practiced, it generally assured a protection of the shareholder by an austere rationing of the gross profits. There was no need within the market system for the managers or directors to worry about the consumer, the employees, creditors who supplied debt capital, suppliers, or the public. The market mechanism was supposed to take care of each of these, except the last, and it was incumbent upon the manager to make sure that he always drove a hard bargain when negotiating with each of them. In the case of the public, the corporation owed it nothing except taxes and the continuation of effective wealth-generating operations.

The early United States corporate view of the dynamics of the market system was a somewhat expanded version of the rudiments of classical economics. It was generally believed that the competitive market automatically yielded these advantages to the society:[3]

1. Lowest possible cost in production and distribution of goods and services
2. Minimum profits
3. Allocation of energy and materials and capital to those goods and services that the public wanted, and in proportion to their demands
4. Return to each factor in production in harmony with its contribution to the public
5. Constant effort to widen the choice of goods and services offered
6. Constant effort to improve the goods offered
7. Assured freedom of opportunity to start a business if capital was available
8. Continuous progress and gradually improving scale of living

There was no "dividend retention" decision to be made under nineteenth-century corporate accountability. All net earnings after taxes were a return on the owners' capital and went directly to them. It was up to the owners to reinvest their returns at the point where the next return on capital was optimum. Furthermore, the managers were not to be consciously concerned with such intangibles as corporate "growth," corporate prestige, charitable contributions, and social responsibility. If these intangible claims were answered by successful and profitable performance, that was fine; but they were not to be pursued as ends in themselves, and certainly the managers were not to drive up the immediate costs of operating by pursuing them.

This environment bred a manager who devoted himself to a single purpose, and who believed that the market system would soon destroy the inefficient. He also believed in natural liberty in all of its ramifications, and this led to a political conviction that the government and all other factions within the society should "mind its own business," as his corporation did. If the government needed specialized help, he as a citizen could ponder its problems, aid if he could on his own time. But as a businessman, he could not help, nor could his company.

The elementary model of nineteenth-century business accountability was essentially the same as the corporate model of that era. In both cases, the owners felt the same form of responsibility. In the corporate case, the manager clearly understood his rigorous accountability to easily identifiable owners.

4 Erosion of Accountability

Economic man or woman seems to be made mostly of straw.
—STUART CHASE, in *The Social Responsibilities of Management,* 1950

In England, at some time in the middle years of the nineteenth century, a new school of liberals became articulate. They recoiled at the excesses of the young European capitalism, at the abuses of human beings in the mines and mills. They would inexorably replace the earlier "nineteenth-century liberals" as their movement grew. Their growth presaged the general decline of the philosophy of natural liberty, the coming erosion of the Protestant Ethic, the weakening of ownership, and the advent of collectivism.

The late Joseph Schumpeter,[1] the brilliant Austrian-American economist, and many others writing subsequently, saw a defect in the classic model of "perfect" competition. Although the classical economists had demonstrated that the search for profits was compatible with maximum beneficial production in society, they had not demonstrated a direct correlation between the two. And the flaw lay in their construction of the model for competition. With some over-simplification, it can be said that Schumpeter felt that perfect competition was based upon a myopic short-run view, had never been feasible, nor had ever existed, and that it

31

was particularly unfeasible and undesirable in powerful modern economies. He saw perfect competition, with its many small firms, as a completely inadequate model in a world in which large-scale establishments were not a necessary evil, but a positive requirement to foster technological progress in production. He concurred in the view of competition as a regulator, but only in a long-term framework. Progress comes from innovation, and innovation springs from large economic units operating in the hope of gaining a monopoly position; the regulative force originates in the next innovator, who will aspire and act toward his own monopoly position.

In the early years of the twentieth century, "perfect" competition was becoming a hopelessly inapplicable concept, both for defining what was happening and what was needed for valid regulation. Also, a more fundamental attack was made on the impersonal, mechanistic regulation that was supposed to come from competition working in the market system. Within the microspheres of their corporations, and also generally throughout their society and government, Americans began to believe in the fully rational approach. They could *plan* for profits within the company, and adequate planning would ensure results. They could *engineer* innovation and progress on predictable, almost routine schedules. As this rationalism grew, willingness to rely upon Adam Smith's "invisible hand" as a regulator decayed, and "planning" became a term used with growing frequency in the macrosphere of economics.

In this great questioning process, one of the three crucial inputs to the market system, the regulation afforded by perfect competition, was being cast into doubt, and the other required inputs were also under attack.

The market system had assumed an ever-functioning acquisitive man, a perpetual "maximizer of profits," a creature who became known as "economic man." The businessman, in adopting this creation of the economists, became one of the few human agents in history, if not the only one, who frankly professed an egoistic or self-seeking creed. This creed, from its inception, was always in conflict with one of the basic tenets of the Judaeo-Christian ethic and other religions; namely, that self-denial and selflessness are the servants of the common good.

However, economic man betrayed weakness on other than moral grounds. The comprehensive study of industrial workers at the Hawthorne Works of the Western Electric Company from 1927 to 1932, carried out by Professor Elton Mayo of the Harvard Business School and his staff, became a landmark along the route to a concept of social man. Mayo's work led to a demonstrable case against the concept of economic man, for he proved the response of workers to noneconomic conditions. In the succeeding years, psychology, sociology, and comparative anthropology would continue to remodel the nineteenth-century concept and the individualism in which it was founded.

How did the Ethic, which had motivated nineteenth-century man, fare in the cooling climate? Two recent observers have collected many diverse trends into a compelling account of the decay of the Ethic in modern United States. William H. Whyte, Jr., of *Fortune* magazine, and Professor David Riesman of Harvard have painted widely accepted portraits of the organization man and the "other-directed man."[2] Both types are hypersensitive to the expectations of other humans in their environment, and both fit well into the world that some social scientists now foresee. Whyte constructs the outlines of a new social ethic that may govern modern Western man and under which the pressures of organized society upon the individual are justified.

Two bastions of the market system have been discussed

and found weakened. This leaves one of the crucial three—
the consumer who is both willing and able to exercise his
preference in the market place. Here, again, there is attack
and erosion. To summarize much current commentary, it
may be said that, first, superaggressive salesmanship has
robbed the consumer of his initiative, that is, he can be, and
is being, manipulated. Second, as technology races on, the
consumer is increasingly less competent to judge quality or
to communicate what he wants in terms of what the laboratory can give him. It is also charged that in our affluent
society, the consumers' vote is no longer effective in determining the ends to which production factors should be
committed.

Along with the market system and the Ethic, the broad
political philosophy of natural liberty also came under cor-
rosive attack. The ancient theory of natural law held that
right and wrong could be established by reasoning from the
nature of man. It led to a theory of the sovereignty of the
people, to a concept that any political sovereign cannot do
certain things without contradicting the very reason for its
existence. The stream of democratic thought stemmed from
natural law, from Aristotle, John Locke, Jefferson, and Marshall. Another opposite stream of thought, articulated long
ago by Thomas Hobbes, spoke for an absolute sovereignty.
After 1900 new legal theories came into being in the United
States, and were put into practice, which leaned away from
natural law and toward Hobbes.[3] Corporate law moved in
the same pattern, and there were growing limitations on the
owner's use and disposition of his property, and on freedom
of contract. The process has been termed *the socialization
of law*.

The foregoing analysis shows some of the trends that
differentiate the present century from the preceding one
and which have contributed to the weakening of the ac-

countability to ownership. The changes can be described as evolution or revolution, depending on the observer's value system.

Decline of Ownership

> Ownership has been separated from control; and this separation has removed many of the checks which formerly operated to curb the abuse of wealth and power. And, as ownership of the shares is becoming increasingly dispersed, the power which formerly accompanied ownership is becoming increasingly concentrated in the hands of a few.—
> MR. JUSTICE BRANDEIS, dissenting, in *Louis K. Liggett Co. v. Lee* (1933)

The Boston Manufacturing Company, formed in 1813 with eleven shareholders, represented a beginning in multiple ownership. What has happened to the ownership of corporations from 1813 to the present? There are excellent data to show how many shares of corporate stock are owned and how many are exchanged; reasonably good data estimate share ownership of the large investment institutions. But little reliable information with regard to who owns how much stock in the United States, and in particular, with regard to the degree of concentration of stock ownership in relation to the *control* of corporations. In fact, the term *control*, although widely used in the literature, is itself susceptible to varying definitions.

The decline of ownership as a force is chiefly a result of the decline of *concentration* of share ownership, or the decline of the percentage of a company's total equity owned by any identifiable group or individual. It may be assumed that as the total number of shareholders increases, concentration decreases; and since the rapid increase in the number of shareholders in the nation is well established, the trend is obvious. The vigorous program, sometimes called "people's capitalism," instituted nine years ago by the New York Stock Exchange has been bearing fruit. Its objective is 22 million United States shareholders by 1970, a reasonable goal. The 1962 census of shareholders gave the following facts:

In 1962 there were an estimated 17,010,000 Americans who owned stock in publicly-held U.S. corporations. This was more than 2½ times the 1952 total, almost twice the 1956 total, and 35% above the 1959 total.

1 out of 6 U.S. adults is now a shareholder.

The median age of new shareholders since 1959 is 39, compared to a median age of 48 for all shareholders.

In 1959, 10.7% of the total shareholders were members of labor unions.

The U.S. Dept. of Labor classification *Proprietors, Managers, & Officials,* although relatively a small group, accounts for 2,276,000 holders, or 14% of the total.[4]

These data indicate how many Americans are concerned to any extent (that is, own at least one share) in the ownership of United States corporations. Significantly, there is no information here concerning concentration of ownership.

A sophisticated attempt was made by the Brookings Institution in 1945 to determine concentration of share owning.[5] Unfortunately, this work refers largely to the prewar period 1937–1939. However, the data are still informative:

In 176 selected large corporations, the 20 largest stockholders owned 23.8% of the market value of the common stock. In the Manufacturing companies only, this figure was 25.8%.

Of the 176 large corporations, in 58 companies representing 43.8% of the total assets of the group, no dominant stockholding group could be identified.

In this study, where a "dominant" group was found, the extent of influence of this group was not interpretable. It required several assumptions before the Brookings study could reach its conclusions:[6]

1. Probably less than one-fifth of the common stock of the selected large companies was owned, in 1937–1939, by individuals or groups in a position to exercise a strong influence on management.

2. The mere existence and size of some substantial minority holdings tell little or nothing of the extent to which stockholding groups actually participate in the function of business leadership.

In 1960, Standard and Poor's Corporation examined ownership concentration in listed corporations.[7] Here the search was for "large holdings" in management, defined as beginning at 20 per cent and continuing up to 80 per cent. A list of 150 companies in which large management holdings exist was published. One informative conclusion can be drawn from this investigation: It is significant that the 150 companies, although they are for the most part listed on the stock exchanges, are not among the largest companies.

Ten eminent bankers, who were consulted about concentration of share ownership, answered in agreement and may be paraphrased: "In the banking business, we now define 'substantial ownership' as 2% or more of the outstanding common stock. Even with this definition, we rarely find substantial ownership in the modern corporate world."

In the same vein, many senior corporate officers who were interviewed said that no concentration of their company's stock as high as 1 per cent was in the hands of any group or individual. All interviewees confirmed that highly diffused ownership is a fact of this era, though in the case of the younger corporations, of course, substantial and active ownership groups are still alive.

A rigorous study that would disclose the extent of diffusion of stock ownership could be made, but no one has done it. The fact of extensive dispersion and the decline of concentration, however, is obvious. Ownership, once a simple quality with simply defined prerogatives, has become in the corporate world a quality that is hard to find, difficult to identify, too complicated to define. It is a framework of prerogatives that must be legalistically interpreted. It is no longer taken for granted as an anchor to legitimacy.

5 Twentieth-Century Model

Religion and law and creeds ought never to be made subjects of discussion by your majesty, for these are the concerns of prophets, not the business of Kings. . . . From the days of Adam until now they have been the mission of prophets and apostles, as rule and government have been the duty of Kings. . . . My advice is that your majesty should never talk about these matters.—Advice to a sixteenth-century Indian sultan from his counselor. Quoted by ARNOLD TOYNBEE, in *A Study of History*

In the successive economic shocks of the early 1930s, business leaders began to propose modifications of the inherited concepts of business responsibility. These modifications, and their subsequent refinements under the spur of a massive regulatory government, led to practices in corporate management that portended a new structure of accountability—an antithesis of the earlier form. Modern managers tend to maintain roots in the old accountability while seeking to adopt portions of the new concepts in widely varying degrees. The new model can be pictured for the use of the manager who wishes to approach it or avoid it.

Long before 1929, the stage had been set. Henry Ford, one of America's great businessmen, although a strict puritan, was never an economic man. He was profoundly motivated by factors outside the market place—by his desire to use the machine as a new messiah that would lighten the burdens of the workingmen and the farmers of the world. He established the thoroughly unclassical concept that blended the employee and the customer into one man. In 1914 he implemented an unprecedented (and again unclassical) management practice when he declared to his board of directors that his company would henceforth pay $5.00 in wages for an eight-hour day.[1] He was a pillar of ownership, but he would not act in the market place according to the old precepts of ownership. The men of his age who tried to share ownership with him, as shareholders in his company, were often violently in disagreement with him.

Ford's own concept of corporate accountability was broader than that of the nineteenth-century model, which still prevailed. In 1919, when he tried to share profits with customers by sharply reducing prices, he was confronted by a fact of law that is still true today. His shareholders sued him, and the trial judge upheld them when he stated unequivocally that a business corporation is organized and carried on primarily for the profit of the shareholders. Also, the court said that the directors could not lawfully "conduct the affairs of a corporation for the merely incidental benefit of the shareholders, and for the primary purpose of benefitting others. . . ."[2]

But businessmen would persist in thinking ahead of the law. One of the early signs of cleavage in professional management thinking was revealed in a speech by Owen D. Young, then chairman of the General Electric Company, in an address in 1929. Young spoke of the conflict he felt in choosing between two roles. In the first role, the director was an attorney for the shareholder, retained by the shareholder and devoted to his interests. In the second role, he was a trustee for the corporate institution, and as a trustee he had *several* responsibilities. The first was to the providers of capital, to whom he owed the safe use of their capital and an adequate return for its use. But he also had obligations to the employees of his institution, to the customers it served, and to the society and government in which it existed. By implication, these responsibilities were nearly equal in importance, or at least any one of them might be subordinated to the others at a given time.

In these remarks, Young professed his leaning toward the latter of the two roles, and he became one of the first businessmen to talk openly of *multiple objectives*. Also, for the first time, a business manager had spoken seriously of an old concept that was now to become the crux of the accountability problem—the concept of social responsibility.

In the early 1930s, the Swope plan was formed to induce American business to take the lead in implementing "social responsibility," to head off drastic government intervention in business. In the years after World War II, the concept of the business manager's social responsibility was refined. Its most articulate spokesman was Frank Abrams, chairman of the Standard Oil Company of New Jersey. Management was viewed as the arbitrator who determines the "balanced best interests" of the several publics of the corporation. This role of arbitrator, or social umpire, was defined many times in the management literature of the 1950s. Generally, the manager's responsibility was delineated as stewardship of the best interests of his corporation's shareholders, customers, employees, its industry, and of its governments, community, and suppliers. In the world of big government, big labor, and big business, this was big stewardship.

The decay of the nineteenth-century rationales placed American corporate managers in the middle of a conflict between old and new philosophies. In the resulting strains, it is not surprising that a schism developed in managerial outlook. Observers noted that the American business creed was split into two versions: the classical version, which held to the precepts of nineteenth-century economics, and the managerial version, which developed a more adaptive view.[3] The latter view was that inside the corporation, ownership is no longer the link to legitimacy of authority. Authority comes from the hierarchy, and ownership is the subsequent reward for demonstrated management virtue, via the route of the stock option. For years, capital has not been the fruit of individual savings that are invested and reinvested wisely by economic men; capital is the stream of internally generated funds within the company, or is the result of financially ingenious and rigorous compulsions to save, such as pension plans or life insurance policies. Meanwhile, the former simple accountability to ownership has been diffracted. The modern corporate manager finds it difficult to keep track of all the fragments of constraining influences that now surround him, and to all of which he is answerable at some time and in some manner.

Outside the company, in the macrosphere of the economic society, the modern manager generally reverts to the classical version. Ownership, represented in the aggregate by the shareholders, is still the public anchor for the legitimacy of authority, in the view of the majority of managers. Competition in the market place, under whatever theory it may operate, is still the regulator and must be preserved. Planning, or economic engineering to enhance the workings of the national economy, is generally regarded as antithetical to the interests of the economic process. Hence, planning in the economic macrosphere at times brings forth a hostile response from managers. It is interesting to note that American managers always assume that macrosphere economic planning will be done by some men, or some institutions, other than management.

With this background, the twentieth-century model of corporate accountability can be outlined.[4] As implied earlier, it is a model that is being approached in widely varying degrees by contemporary corporations. The hired manager, in the form of a chief executive officer without substantial stockholding in the company, occupies a pivotal position in the new structure. He has no single orientation in answerability, as formerly; rather he is oriented toward the directors and the several groups who are contributors to, or claimants on, the company. There is no pyramidal structure here, with a "top," and the analyst is immediately reduced to the position of the political philosophers of the seventeenth century who tried to chase down *sovereignty* to its ultimate location.[5] The arrangement is not linear, but circular, and in reality there is no sovereignty. Hence the statement that the corporate chief executive officer[6] is at the pivotal location. He is senior, and thereby most accountable, within the corporate structure, and he dispenses the benefits from the corporation's work to the shareholders, the customers, the employees, the business community and his suppliers, and to the community at large. Yet he is dependent upon these publics in the aggregate, and he can be deposed by their displeasures, combined in any of many proportions.

In this structure, the corporation is still a private organization (with its stock publicly held), and by the economists' classification, it is still in the private sector of the economy. But the old conviction that each group in the society, including the government, should "mind its own business" is missing. The corporate leaders are concerned with large issues of public policy, with the health of their industry, and with the health of the economy of the United States. They are vitally concerned with the health of supranational economic organizations, such as the European coal and steel community, or Euratom. Management now regards public policy as an area in which it has a right to intervene and a duty to aid in formulation of that policy by lobbying, testifying before public bodies, and using other political techniques. Governmental agencies are regarded as suppliers of required services, such as law and order or public education; they are also important customers.

In the twentieth-century accountability, management never absolves itself of moral responsibility by stressing the fact of control by impersonal market forces. It attempts generally to assume social responsibility for its actions, and at times presumes to be philanthropic. The existence of power within corporations, and over employees and suppliers, presents ethical questions that have not been fully answered, nor have they ever been in the history of human institutions. In this model of present accountability, however, management develops an internal government that it believes to be compatible with the ideal of the democratic environment. For example, it ceases to regard labor as merely a factor of production, and will in time evolve some scheme of relationship with unions that will circumscribe conflict.

In this form of accountability, management subscribes to advanced hypotheses in the development of social perception. A few years ago, the prevailing concept was *participation*, which meant that the employee could contribute more than he was contributing to the corporate efforts and should be allowed to do so. But now the ideal is broader and may be labeled *fulfillment*; this means that the employee is capable of being much more than he is and the corporation should therefore develop him to his full potential. Management approaches some form of constitutionalism in which democratic process and suffrage are instilled in varying degrees within its government. It may demand lifelong loyalty from its people, and in turn may grant them protection, security, status, even diversion, education, and other noneconomic perquisites. In short, the corporation becomes a lesser society, a private government.

This twentieth-century model of accountability is an amorphous concept, still in the process of construction and containing some nonsense, some valid roots and some obsolescent roots from classical economics, and some constructive response to changing conditions. It is indeed a difficult structure of answerability to live by—an intolerable burden for the conscientious manager who really tries to assume it.

PART II

Not only does Law in civilized society presuppose
ethical commitment; it presupposes the
existence of a broad area of human conduct
controlled only by ethical norms and not
subject to Law at all. . . .

—Chief Justice Earl Warren, 1962

6 Outside and Inside Views

I . . . note that our key private decision-makers are in a fundamentally exposed position ideologically, and that the more sophisticated of them well know it.—JOHN P. LEWIS, 1962, in a speech prior to his appointment to the President's Council of Economic Advisers

There is a remarkable difference in the concept of prevailing corporate accountability held by those who observe the corporate sphere from the outside (the opinion formers, whose views are generally expressed publicly) and the concept held by those within the corporations, whose views are customarily expressed privately.

In the recent literature, there have been outright allegations that the managers of major United States corporations are accountable to no one. These charges are couched in temperate language and can be differentiated from the usual demagogic attacks that business leaders have been conditioned to ignore. It is the purpose here to consider these charges, and excerpts from them will be quoted in order to allow the reader to sample their content more directly.

The first voice to be considered belongs to the grandfather of the critics of accountability, Adolf A. Berle, Jr., eminent attorney and student of the law, professor, board chairman, copious author, and New Deal political administrator.[1] His thirty-five years of work have indeed shed light on the status of accountability in United States corporations. He has pointed out the rapid emergence of the investment institution as the great owner of the modern business world. With respect to this emergence, he wrote:

Two things can happen. One, more or less absolute power can be frozen in the corporate managements. Two, the institutional trustees can themselves freeze onto this power. But in either case, the traditional role of responsibility is being eliminated. We no longer will have a group of financially-interested stockholders to which each corporate management must account.[2]

Defining *control* as "quite simply the capacity to make or unmake a board of directors," Berle portrayed four phases:

Phase 1. *Absolute* control, represented by the family companies.

Phase 2. *Working* control, where there is a close bond between a few strong elements of ownership and the members of the board of directors.

Phase 3. *Management* control, where the board regularly expects the majority of shareholders to follow their lead.

Phase 4. Here the fiduciary institution emerges, and dispersed shareholding once again tends to become concentrated. Voting power becomes concentrated in these institutions, while beneficial ownership is even more widely dispersed to the beneficiaries of the institution (for example, members of a pension trust).

Berle's implications should be regarded as indicative of widespread opinion outside the corporations. His first conclusion was that the established separation of ownership from control was making the managers free of restraints from owners and from the edicts of the classical market system. Next, this freedom from older constraints was leading to changes in managers' behavior and in corporate performance. Finally, these effects were becoming increasingly important because the assets of the United States were becoming more concentrated in the hands of these large corporations.

Another commentator on corporate accountability is Ernest Dale, professor at the Cornell graduate business school and management consultant in New York. He remarked in an address before the American Economic Association in December, 1960:

But, if we are to be true to our most fundamental traditions, we must insist that power have some place to which it is answerable. As it is well known, this tradition is not being honored. Increasingly the top managements of large corporations are beholden to themselves alone.[3]

Carl Kaysen, professor of economics at Harvard, writes often in this vein:

In the evolving giant corporation, managers possess great scope for decision-making unconstrained by market forces, and nowhere more so than in their decisions with respect to future growth and change. . . . Formally speaking, management in making these decisions is responsible only to itself. . . .[4]

Edward S. Mason of Harvard states:

What Mr. Berle and most of the rest of us are afraid of is that this powerful corporate machine, which so successfully grinds out the goods we want, seems to be running without any discernible controls. The young lad mastering the technique of his bicycle may legitimately shout with pride, "Look, Ma, no hands," but is this the appropriate motto for a corporate society?[5]

Gerard Swope, former president of the General Electric Company, is quoted that he

agrees that directors and stockholders provide no practical curbs on management. . . . Management today does define its own responsibilities. It depends on the personal factor of the president in each case. It depends on whether he is selfish and narrow or broad and has a sense of stewardship.[6]

John P. Lewis of Indiana University, in an address in 1962 to the White House Conference on National Economic

Issues, and prior to his appointment to the President's Council of Economic Advisers, put the charge in these words:

. . . far from being the impersonal market mechanism of the economics text books, the present system concentrates in relatively few private hands discretionary authority to make decisions of major economy-wide impact. And it contains little in the way of explicit accountability mechanisms for rendering these key wielders of private power responsible to the public.

Ben W. Lewis, chairman of the Department of Economics at Oberlin College, wrote in the *Harvard Business Review*:

In significant proportions, society's economizing decisions are made, out of hand, by relatively few people who sit above the market in key positions within huge conglomerates of economic power.[7]

The literature abounds with more examples of the conclusion, drawn with some air of finality, that top management accountability is nil. Congressmen, retired executives, and academicians have jumped on this rolling bandwagon. A common thread runs through these allegations. The general theme is the loss of accountability; the specific theme is the charge of irresponsible or potentially irresponsible use of the society's economic resources by those in power within the corporation microspheres.

There is another school of criticism presently growing, from which charges of lack of accountability are also leveled at corporate managers. This new sortie, not yet well articulated, is framed in the area of the internal government of the large corporation. Its framers believe that power is used within the corporate government in a way that "substantially violates the prevailing values of American democracy."[8] They also note that the corporation may be the "school of political prudence in which we learn not to practice what the political republic has always preached."[9]

At this point it is appropriate to consider the inside view, expressed with equal conviction by managers who must exercise accountability within the corporations.

The Inside View

> No matter what a man's general education or his adult education for management, what will be decisive above all . . . is neither education nor skill; it is integrity of character.
> —PETER F. DRUCKER in *The Practice of Management*, 1954

Business leaders in the Western world are currently preoccupied with the total nature and the effects in the aggregate of the constraints upon their decision-making processes. In the 1960s, there are no remnants in the managerial outlook of the theory that the forces in the market system completely determine a manager's strategic reactions. But these simple, powerful forces have been replaced by a host of complex powerful forces, economic and noneconomic in nature. Industrial executives, financial institution officers, and consultants with whom I discussed accountability in connection with this writing believed that the moral responsibility of large business had "immeasurably," "substantially," "many-times" improved since the days of the depression, and they were willing to concede that external regulative forces counted for much in this improvement.

The major constraining forces identified by top corporate managements are listed below, with emphasis upon the first five as the most important. They are distilled from the remarks of many senior executives:

1. *Effects of competition* (however the economists may classify the type of competition) are a powerful and perpetual constraint. The competitive forces are vigorous, and acting in the areas of price-cost relationships, share of market, innovation and new products, product reliability, and the substitution of one good or service for another.

2. *Inward accountability* is a required quality in a senior executive. The long-term effects of professional management training, long process of selection and survival, and arduous performance demands have produced a breed of top executives who are in 99 per cent of the cases morally responsible, effective, and can be entrusted with the power required at the helm of a modern corporation. The bearer of this power feels acutely not only the consciousness of fiduciary duty in the heritage of the trustee but also the strong and growing new force in the constraints of the profession of management.

3. *Necessity to please the shareholders and their analysts,* by adequate performance (the crucial ingredient) and in countless minor ways. Shareholders may not usually be a force, but they are an ever-present spirit. Their displeasure can always damage a company's reputation, and at times when equity capital is sought in the market, this displeasure can be directly expensive. The sharply growing number of analysts and the growing holdings of sophisticated investment institutions make this a demanding task.

4. *Recognition by one's peers* is a powerful influencing force. In the "political world" in which top managers live, their achievements and their mistakes become readily known to the whole world-wide fraternity of peers. The approval of this group for effective performance is a meaningful reward; its censure for ineffective performance is to be avoided.

5. *Necessity to build a positive structure of personnel relations* in their companies, with all employees, from the professional to the unskilled, organized or unorganized.

6. *Demands of the federal corporate income tax;* the requirement to respond intelligently to its provisions, however distorting they may be to the economizing process, in all aspects of financial planning and control.

7. *Compliance with national and state legislation;* antitrust, labor, and other laws.

8. The demanding concept of *service to the customers,* beyond their immediate and minimum needs.

9. *Regulations of the Securities and Exchange Commission* requiring full disclosure, appropriate handling of shareholder proposals, rigorous voting procedures, and other provisions.

10. *Regulations of the several stock exchanges* governing listed companies.

11. *Necessity for favorable relations with the suppliers of long-term debt capital,* and in many cases with the providers of working capital obtained by short-term borrowing.

12. *Continuous maintenance* of a *capability* to serve those civil and military agencies that determine the needs and purchasing policies of the federal government.

13. *Maintenance* of a *favorable posture* generally in the whole community: with educational institutions, civic groups, charitable agencies, trade associations, scientific and engineering associations, management groups, and others.

14. *Necessity for maintaining positive relations* with all key suppliers who provide materials, services, and equipments.

15. *Constructive fear* of *stockholders' derivative suits* ("strike" suits), and beyond that the specter of the corporate raider.

Modern industrial leaders keenly feel an all-pervading sense of competition. Nowhere is the gulf between academician and practitioner wider or more opaque. The executives have never understood the terminology of the elaborate structure that has been built over the old, nonexistent "perfect" competition. Such terms as "oligopolistic competition" or "quasi-monopolistic competition" have a useful meaning only within the esoteric confines of academic institutions.

These constraining influences will be considered again in

later pages. It is their comprehensive sum that now troubles the more discerning members of top corporate management. The significant problems under current evaluation are these:

1. Do these constraints in the aggregate constitute a form of overcontrol, to the point where our industrial virility and innovative power are jeopardized? Or are these constraints in the aggregate insufficient to protect industry from the shallow or dishonest self-interest seeker who has lodged himself in the management institution at a point of influence in an important corporation?

2. Do these constraints in the aggregate positively induce management behavior and management decisions that are in keeping with the needs and wants of the society, needs that include both "economic performance" and "social justice"?

3. In the negative sense, does the cumulative effect of the constraints prevent socially and economically undesirable management performance?

4. How do we find the answers to the questions posed above? Is there any scheme at all for the understanding and analysis of the cumulative effects of accountability in United States corporate management?

Financial Accountability as It Now Exists

> The South Sea Company . . . had an immense capital . . . an immense number of proprietors. It was naturally to be expected, therefore, that folly, negligence, and profusion should prevail in the whole management of their affairs.—
> ADAM SMITH, *Wealth of Nations,* 1776

If corporate managements are now changing their behavior patterns for the worse, this unhappy fact should show up first in the financing trends of their corporations. Earnings might be retained at an increasing rate for expansion and operations, with resultant freedom of managements from the capital market system. However, informed opinion[10] now holds that there has been only a slight increase in the use of internally generated funds during the past sixty years. The long-term trends confirm the increased use of depreciation allowance, offset by a decreased use of retained earnings.[11] This long-term slight increase must be interpreted reasonably: Has it resulted from managerial grasping for more internal earnings as an escape route from the money market, or is it a less sinister development stemming naturally from the steadily increasing fixed assets in United States corporations? Management must render clear its own position with respect to its accountability for the use of economic resources, and in so doing, it should consider some recent evidence of further slight increases in use of internal funds since 1950 in the financing of corporations.[12]

It also might have been predicted that managements would reduce the dividend rate as they came into this era of alleged new freedoms. Lintner[13] in 1956 made a statistical study of the dividend practices of corporations from 1918–1940 and found that his formulas for those years could accurately predict dividend practices in 1945–1951. In other words, the pattern of dividend performance has not changed.

Then there is also the question of the non-owning status of managements. This "deficiency" may cause managements to *respond* inadequately or sluggishly to changes in the cost of capital, that is, not use this market in shrewd self-interest in the way of nineteenth-century economic man. If this were true, it would mean that the allocative function of this market—the placing of capital where it would do the most good for the society—was being bypassed. But it is not true. In recent years, as in earlier years, corporations have alternated in the use of stocks and bonds, in accordance with variations in the relative cost of capital by equity or debt financing.[14] Managements have conformed to the market; they have driven the best deal for capital within the limitations of their knowledge and experience, as did the owner-managers of earlier generations.

Since internal funds provide for more than 60 per cent of their fund needs, it may also be alleged that corporations are bypassing one of the most important allocaters, the one by which savings are directed via profit indicators to those producing units that turn out the goods most wanted in the society. Management with its freedom may be simply financing the new projects that happen to be available.

But neither will this charge stand up to the light of investigation. A study[15] covering the past twenty-five years in several industries shows that the industries having the greatest expansion in plant and equipment have been the same ones having the greatest growth in profits and earning the highest rates of profits. Also, the comprehensive recent study by Edwin Kuh of M.I.T.[16] of 700 companies in the 1946–1950 period details the investment policies in seventeen different manufacturing industries. The conclusion was that the current rate of investment in all these companies was determined by (1) rate of profits, (2) sales level, and (3) the relation between sales level and manufacturing capacity. These two studies indicate that investment funds are still flowing in the channels where profit is to be found.

In one more area there have been repeated expressions of alarm. Writers have tended to use the term *growing concentration* as almost one word, and a commonly accepted picture is one of steadily increasing assets in the hands of the large corporations. It is not a true picture, as most scholars have agreed by now. M. A. Adelman of M.I.T. did his classical study on industrial concentration in 1951 and updated it in 1958.[17] As indices of concentration he used sales, income generated, share of total employment, and share of national income-producing wealth, or assets. His general conclusions were that, first, the American economy is highly concentrated, and second, the concentration is highly uneven from industry to industry. Third, and most significantly for present purposes, concentration in American industry shows no tendency to increase, and perhaps some tendency to decline. Since early in this century it has moved, if at all, at the speed of "a glacial drift." The nation's assets are not inexorably being gulped into the maw of the large corporations.

There is a conclusion here relevant to the study of accountability. The managers *are* answerable to the demands of their society, as expressed in economic dimensions by the mechanism of the markets. The extent of this accountability is surely open to further questioning, and managers will agree that they can learn to conform even more closely to the constraints of the market and thereby improve their demonstration of accountability. No analyst will dissect this structure of accountability to determine which type of constraints upon management are effective or to identify the manner in which they constrain. It is quite conceivable that the internal, self-imposed restraints of the better managements may contribute a great deal to the successfully accountable economic performance. In the aggregate, the constraints are effective and do result in socially desirable performance in the economic dimension.

Managers would do well, however, not to read too much into this fact. If managements can demonstrate that they are as accountable as their forefathers were, at least in the crucial economic dimension, then why the voluminous allegations about lack of accountability from intelligent sources? And why the lack of a clarifying response from management?

7 The Shareholder's Role

> . . . attitudes toward legitimacy are among the important motivations that produce acceptance of authority. Authority that is viewed as legitimate is not felt as coercion or manipulation, either by the man who exercises it, or by the man who accepts it.—HERBERT A. SIMON in *Research in Industrial Human Relations*[1]

What is the real function of the holder of voting stock in the United States corporate scene? As an individual and as an institution, the shareholder has been viewed from different quarters in several different lights: as the provider of capital for corporate equity financing; the wielder of the power of ownership who replaces the old proprietors and furnishes policy guidance for operating managements; the potential saviour of the corporation from managements who are allegedly unaccountable; or the spirit of ownership, which provides legitimacy for the corporation and breathes into it the dynamics of a private economic organization.

Corporate leaders are now beginning to understand that the role of the shareholder has undergone a profound change.[2] Ownership in the corporate environment is now a simulated quality, although still an important and constructive one. This synthetic position brings some of the tangible and intangible rewards of the old ownership to shareholders, but it also brings legitimacy to corporate managements. Thus the shareholder is the agent of legitimacy for management, and as such he is deserving of deferential treatment. As the number of shareholders grows, these agents become more dispersed throughout the population, and are therefore more representative of the population. The anchor to legitimacy is thereby strengthened, even though such growth further dilutes ownership.

Along with legitimacy in the eyes of the law and the public, the shareholder gives to the large business corporation the priceless mantle of the *private institution*. This corporation, and its management, are thereby sheltered in the microsphere from the full extent of the governmental regulation that falls upon the public institutions, such as the large federal and state agencies and the semipublic institutions such as the New York Port Authority. This mantle may well be the most valuable possession of modern management in large business corporations because it retains for it entrepreneurial latitude and freedom.

Although management fully recognizes this indebtedness to the American stockholder, it is at the same time in the position of only rarely being able to heed the stockholders' advice. One is reminded of the king in a modern monarchy who enjoys the adulation and deference of his populace, draws his stipends, presides at certain ceremonies, but yet is courteously ignored should he ever indiscreetly venture near the parliament. However, wherever recognizable blocks of stock are held by an individual or a small cohesive group, some degree of direct owner control is exerted. This situation is found less and less frequently in large corporations as the base of ownership is steadily eroded by the attrition of the estate tax, the antitrust laws, and the process of dilution through growth. Yet it still exists in some places, and it serves to illustrate that the accountability of ownership is currently a matter of some controversy.

The point of controversy is stated in the following thoughts, the first one expressed by the chairman of the board of an international mining company, and the second by a senior management consultant with international recognition:

Chairman: My brother and I still hold about 10 per cent of the stock in this company. But we are the last of the owners—the current president is a hired manager, an engineer who has been with us for years. I sincerely believe that he, and our other officers, feel the same responsibility for this company that I do, by virtue of their office. . . . I suspect that if you pinned me down, I might admit that my owner's sense of responsibility is a little "expanded" over theirs.

Management consultant: Do you imply that the old accountability of ownership was superior to the present accountability, whatever it may be? I can't go along with the sentimentalists who long for the good old days of the big owners. They (the big owners) perpetrated most of the sins for which business is still being crucified daily by all the anti-business factions. Life may have been simpler then, but that's the only good thing I could say about it.

This controversy, centering about the relative merits of proprietary ownership versus managerial control, will not be factually resolved in the near future.[3] There are no complete data that correlate degree of ownership concentration with corporate performance, and the demonstrated effectiveness of shareholder proprietors as operating managers must remain obscure for the time being. Proprietary efficiency, however, is taken for granted by those who advocate a movement known as shareholder democracy. They want to restore to the modern scene the former virtues of managerial accountability to ownership.

Shareholder Democracy: Real or Fanciful?

> If you are going to have a profit, it will be produced by the
> workers and by workers I mean all the people from the
> janitor up to the president. These are the people who should
> be rewarded in proportion to their contribution. The last
> man to reward is the stockholder, particularly the ones who
> have no interest in the company outside the bigger divi-
> dends and the higher price of the stock.—JAMES F. LINCOLN,
> Chairman, Lincoln Electric Company. Address to Sym-
> posium on Productivity in a Free Society, 1962

Americans have always believed along with Aristotle that
virtue can best be defined by the multitude: The many are
more incorruptible than the few. A multitude is a better
judge of many things than any individual.

America in the nineteenth century was a citadel for the
multitude of the voter and also a citadel of ownership. The
share of common stock had two essential prerogatives:
ownership of equity and a *vote*. It was thereby two ways
sacrosanct. Very early, the line of reasoning grew: The shareholder *owns*; therefore he *controls*. Strategic decisions, like
the disposition of net earnings after taxes, are his.

When ownership and management were essentially the
same, there were few problems. Even so, the idea of shareholder control, as often expressed then and now, was probably always a delusion. In law, the shareholders' "control"
was the capacity to make or unmake the board of directors.
Beyond that, he had few rights in control, other than to
resort to the courts if he was displeased (the derivative
suit).

But the delusion has persisted in the movement now
called shareholder democracy by its sponsors. Its advocates
are voices crying in the wilderness, but they are sustained
by the force of their convictions and probably in some cases

by their desire to exploit the leadership of a popular movement. One of the most sincere proponents was the late William Z. Ripley of Harvard, whose stand in the 1930s can be surmised from one of his chapter titles,[4] "Giving up Control: A Birthright for Pottage."

Ripley was not sure whether the enemy who was bilking the shareholder at the time was management (the archvillain of present writings by the shareholder democrats) or the banker (the archvillain of earlier days). But he shared one conviction with his present-day descendants—stockholders must organize. He noted shrewdly that labor in the United States had lost as long as it allowed management to deal with employees individually. Collective strength was the answer. And collectivism could be achieved by a familiar route, by modifying the board of directors to provide an "independent audit" of management and bankers.

Two facets of Professor Ripley's work should be emphasized here. First, he was astute enough, in contrast to some of his later brethren, to see clearly that shareholder democracy would not and could not work unless the individual shareholder had been educated to be able to assume some minimal *responsibility* in connection with his holdings. He went so far as to propose a permanent agency, governmental or quasi-governmental, that would educate stockholders and induce them to participate intelligently in corporate functions; in his own words, "to make democracy tolerable." Second, he wrote *before* the significant securities legislation of the 1930s.

Every chairman who has presided recently at an annual meeting knows the names of some modern professional shareholders—Lewis and John Gilbert, Wilma Soss, and Benjamin Javits, among others. Businessmen tend to characterize these shareholders in one of three ways: constructive gadflies, dilettantes, or hecklers. The professional shareholders have been complemented by aggressive observers such as Joseph A. Livingston, financial editor of a Philadelphia newspaper, in furthering the rights of the American stockholder.

In the business of shareholder protection, the New York Stock Exchange is the real professional. It has a determined view with regard to the prerogatives of the stockholder, although it has never subscribed to the full-blown aspirations of the shareholder democrats. The Exchange intends to promote stock ownership into the hands of a steadily increasing number of Americans. Its mission is to (1) define and protect the shareholder's *rights*, (2) *educate* him appropriately in the topics he should know so that he can invest and maintain his investment intelligently, and (3) provide for him a *forum* in which all United States shareholders can make known their thinking. The officers of the Exchange well understand, as did Professor Ripley thirty years ago, that the mere broadening of the base of stock ownership, if unaccompanied by any broadened capacities in the new owners, will not necessarily strengthen capitalism.

The ledger book for the present status of management accountability to its shareholders shows both debits and credits, leading to a conclusion that this accountability is reasonably well proscribed in form by the laws, the Securities and Exchange Commission, the stock exchanges, and some remaining traditional forces from the era of ownership. But, in substance, this accountability is badly confused in the understanding of the parties involved. The forms of stockholder protection are so advanced over those prevailing in 1929 that this protection is taken for granted in society. Managements assume that if they neglect the shareholder's rights in any way, they will be reminded immediately of their sin by a regulatory agency.

This may be a form of accountability, but it is no more

than a shadow of the old answerability to the owners of the nineteenth century. Accountability must be positively understood if it is to do the great things for industrial enterprise that it did in its nineteenth-century structure. Although the complex nature of modern administration prohibits a return to the forceful ownership accountability of those years, we must nevertheless find its equivalent in potency and clarity.

The administrative complexity of the modern corporation makes it extremely difficult for the typical individual shareholder to participate constructively or intelligently. The mere enlargement of his franchise, by shareholder democracy or any other means, will not solve the problem. As H. G. Wells pointed out in *The Outline of History*, "Votes in themselves are worthless things. Men had votes in Italy in the time of Gracchi. Their votes did not help them. Until a man has education, a vote is a useless and dangerous thing for him to possess."

The dilemma in which American corporate management finds itself is that it can ill afford to ignore either of the twin forces of shareholder democracy and the New York Stock Exchange's program of people's capitalism. The latter program is succeeding, and fifty or seventy million American shareholders will be strong roots indeed—a powerful dispersion of the anchors of legitimacy for the private corporate institution into the fabric of society. Yet each increment of growth in this program makes shareholder democracy, with its "voters" who would make decisions, so much more unrealistic. The two forces are antithetical, and only the institution of management can resolve them.

The Institutional Investor

> . . . where representatives of a great banking house are on
> the board and are financing the corporation and in close
> relations with the management the policy of the corporation
> is largely determined by the bankers where they choose to
> assume that responsibility.—REPORT OF THE PUJO COM-
> MITTEE, U.S. House of Representatives, 1913[5]

Those critics who would revitalize accountability to the
individual shareholder have watched with mixed feelings
the emergence of a new and powerful force in a shareholding role, that is, the institutional investor.[6] Such critics are
not sure whether this new force will prove to be the saviour
of the individual shareholder or the destroyer of the last
vestiges of his rights to "control."

The institutional investor is of interest here because of a
rather broad change in his status and conduct since 1900
and their effects on corporate accountability. For many
decades, Americans have exhibited an increasing desire to
put aside present income to provide future financial protection for themselves and their families. In their investment
habits, they have relied increasingly upon diversification,
and in recent years upon retaining professional investment
management by various schemes. In their banking habits,
they have demanded greater relative liquidity as their incomes have risen, thereby fostering the large-scale creation
of deposit currency in the banking system.

These tendencies have resulted in a spectacular growth of
the financial intermediaries in the aggregate, and also in
many cases in the creation of new types of intermediaries
such as the mutual fund. During the past fifty years, the
financial intermediaries have been growing (in assets) at a
rate *more than twice as fast* as the growth of all nonfinancial
(industrial, commercial, and mercantile) corporations.[7] In

1955 the total assets of intermediaries were $545 billion, compared with an estimated total assets of nonfinancial corporations of about $500 billion. Before World War I, individuals placed about 40 per cent of their current savings with financial intermediaries; after World War II, more than 80 per cent. About 1900, intermediaries held one-tenth of the entire assets of United States households; at the present, they hold about one-quarter.

Investment institutions have steadily become a more important source of funds for American industry and its nonfinancial corporations. This growth is tabulated in Table 1.

TABLE 1.   Source Capital from Investment Institutions

Period	Approximate Percentage of Total Funds (Debt Plus Equity) Supplied by Intermediaries
1910–1914	35
1920–1929	42
1946–1959	50

Equity financing by intermediaries has grown more erratically, but it has shown a significantly increased rate of growth since 1955. This has resulted in rapidly growing blocks of corporate common stocks in institutional hands, the extent of which will be described shortly.

Many observers have reported that they are concerned about the implications of this trend. Institutional investors, as important providers of funds, may acquire powers of various nature over industrial organizations. In any case, as the institutions acquire common stock, they will absorb the ownership function, thus becoming an insulating block between the investor and the enterprise. Observers see strong concentrating forces at work, moreover, which will affect the voting control of corporations.

Among the institutions that might effect a new distribution of voting control are the mutual investment fund and the noninsured corporate pension fund. Both hold common stocks in large amounts, and both are growing rapidly. The former has been acquiring and holding common stocks in the amounts shown in Table 2.[8]

TABLE 2.   Common Stock Holdings of Open-ended Investment Companies

Year	Percentage of Total New Issues of Common Stock Acquired (Net)	Percentage of Total Holdings of Common Stock Held
1946	7.69	0.90
1947	14.29	1.10
1948	7.69	1.11
1949	12.50	1.33
1950	5.56	1.37
1951	7.41	1.47
1952	12.90	1.77
1953	17.39	1.96
1954	11.54	2.09
1955	16.67	2.18
1956	21.05	2.34
1957	20.00	2.47
1958	23.81	2.75

It is apparent that the mutual funds do not yet own a significant share of the holdings, although they have for years been a buyer of appreciable quantities of the new issues. As a purchaser in the market, the private (non-government) pension funds are also a force to watch, as shown by the figures in Table 3.

This mushrooming stride into common-stock investments by the pension trusts is a comparatively recent development. It started about 1950, when New York State revised its law to allow trustees to place up to 35 per cent of the market value of a trust in common stocks. Also during the 1950s the

TABLE 3.   Stock Holdings of Private Pension Trusts

Year	Percentage of Total New Issues of Common Stock Acquired (Net)	Percentage of Total Holdings of Common Stock Held
1946	7.69	0.3
1947	7.14	0.4
1948	7.69	0.5
1949	6.25	0.6
1950	11.11	0.8
1951	11.11	1.1
1952	16.13	1.5
1953	21.74	2.0
1954	23.08	2.7
1955	23.33	3.5
1956	26.32	4.3
1957	25.00	5.4
1958	28.57	6.7

union-negotiated pension plan covering wage earners became an important factor for the first time.

Common stocks and pension funds were in several ways ideally suited for each other. There was the obvious feature of protecting the fund against inflation and price increases. Funds could enjoy some measure of participation in the growth of the economy as they invested in common stocks. Furthermore, since the projections show a steady increase of pension trusts for many years into the future, there is no need for them to maintain liquidity. The proportion of investment of pension trusts going into common stocks has increased every year since the funds started, and in 1959 passed the 50 per cent mark as the average for all such trusts. The principal bank trustees in New York invest from 35 per cent to 50 per cent of their new funds in common stocks,[9] although one trustee invested 100 per cent in 1958 and 1959. Commercial banks in the United States are also holders of large blocks of common stocks, most of which are held in various kinds of trust arrangements for clients.

Institutional investors in general do not yet own an appreciable percentage of the outstanding common stock, but investment funds and pension funds together are now buying one-half of the new issues of common each year. This fact can be, and often has been, the subject for some interesting speculation about future projections. But first it is necessary to consider what kind of owner these institutions will be.

The general impression, inside and outside business, is that the institutions are actively avoiding any position of power with respect to the companies in which they have large holdings. This attitude is proving a keen disappointment to some observers, particularly to Joseph A. Livingston, a financial editor who recently wrote a book[10] in which he suggested that the institutions become the shepherds for all the small nonprofessional investors, that they aggressively lead the way to a better deal for all shareholders, including the small fry. The professional shareholders are outraged by the passive attitude of the institutional investors, and have repeatedly "called" for a Congressional investigation into the "thousands of institutions" that routinely sign every proxy vote "for" management and "against" the owners.

Institutional investors thus find themselves in a position where they will be actively damned whether they do or they do not. Generally, their primary objectives must be income and capital appreciation, and they cannot afford the costly overheads involved in any general role of the policeman who enforces "good" management. Moreover, such a role would place them in the un-American position of the big absentee landlord—and their managers well remember the TNEC hearings and the earlier hearings before the Pujo committee where government action was aimed at institutional concentrations of ownership.

On the other hand, many institutions are inevitably becoming "substantial" shareholders in large corporations, even though this substantial holding may be limited by practice or regulation to the order of 5 per cent of the outstanding common stock of any company. Further avoidance of "power" or responsibility becomes increasingly awkward, and institutions feel the sting of increasing criticism of their passive role, not only from the sources noted above but also from many other quarters. They cannot much longer resist picking up the baton of authority; and in fact they may have to become "nonstatist civil servants," actively regulating the managements of the corporations. Within the circle of top management of the investing institutions, the attitude of nonintervention is increasingly questioned:

Chairman of the Board, investment fund: This firm is actively trying to re-introduce a long-missing element—a knowledgeable, sophisticated protection of shareholder interests. In this, I tell you frankly that we are *not* typical.

A few years ago, out in the mid-continental part of the United States, there was a large oil company with a very old chief executive. He was a capital featherbedder of the first order. He was also president of an eastern bank, and he had many millions of that company's funds sitting useless on deposit in his bank. We were large shareholders, and very displeased about this, but our "honey" approach didn't work. So we resorted to vinegar. I got together four of the large mutual funds in New York and Boston, and we forced that company to merge with a smaller, tremendously aggressive petroleum company we knew about. The resulting company has really performed, and there's no featherbedding there now.

Most of these banks and insurance companies take the "hands-off" policy because they have conflicting interests involving the same companies in which they hold stock—for example, commercial bank accounts or employee insurance programs. Admittedly, mutual funds have a unique advantage in this respect.

At one of the largest New York commercial banks, an early leader in pension trust administration, the following opinion was stated:

Vice president in charge of pension trust administration: When we vote our common stocks, we are not "rubber stamps," and the commentators who accuse us of this crime disturb us deeply. True, we *generally* adopt the management recommendation, because our very act of investing signifies trust in a particular management. But in any case where we perceive a good reason to question, we question thoroughly, then act if we have to. Here's an example. Last year a large company, in which our funds have substantial holdings, proposed a profit sharing plan for management and certain other employees which we considered unconscionable. We made known our reaction to the management, and then we joined two other large pension fund administrators in a campaign against the management proposal. In the voting, it was defeated.

In another case, a management asked the stockholders to vote to give up their pre-emptive rights on new issues. We declined, and in the ensuing disagreement, we joined again with other administrators to beat the proposal.

I might add that, in both of these cases, the companies involved had large commercial accounts with our banking departments. One of them withdrew its accounts after our trust action, and we thereby lost several million dollars worth of banking business. The problem is that our learned critics do not know of these kinds of actions on our part, and they do not take the trouble to find out.

What do the viewers-with-alarm project as the future result of the increasing growth of the pension funds? First, they see the mechanization of savings, and thereby of investing. By means of life insurance, union pension plans, company pension plans, and investment funds with planned payments, Americans in growing numbers will subscribe to methods that will force them to save, under varying degrees of compulsion. Significantly, these plans all remove the facility of *control* from investment while dispersing to ever greater numbers the *beneficial ownership* involved. The union pension plan member and the mutual fund certificate holder each lack any voice or vote in the final object of their investment. Conversely, their fund administrators gain increasing voting power where common stocks are involved.

Adolf Berle[11] pictures this result in a few years: Several hundred large fund managers will control the one hundred largest industrial and utility corporations. These fund administrators will then have two obvious choices: They can remain passive owners, insulating management and thus allowing management to assume "absolute control." Or, they can absorb this control themselves. Berle and other observers do not like either of these alternatives.

The possibilities of the pension fund managers taking control are real, but the Berle sketch is oversimplified and very probably too pessimistic. True, the assets of the pension funds show a startling growth: They were $6.87 billion in 1951, $22.09 billion in 1958, $32.4 billion in 1961, and $36.0 billion in 1962. True, there is evidence that they concentrate on blue-chip stocks, that they do generally retain this stock indefinitely, and have[12] "effected a substantial net removal of stock from the market." However, John Lintner[13] computed that *if* the pension funds maintained the same concentration of holdings in these issues, *if* the prices of these issues did not rise, and *if* these companies did not issue new stock, then by 1965 the funds as intelligently projected would still own less than 10 per cent of the stock of the blue-chip companies. The *ifs* are very large ones. There is also a definite possibility that the SEC will step in with diversification requirements that will limit the amount of any one company's common stock held by a pension fund, similar to the existing SEC requirements for mutual funds.

It is difficult to make a convincing case that the investment institutions will revitalize shareholder democracy in the nation, nor will they take over control of American industry within a few years. They may be expected, however, to provide on an increasing scale a tough-minded, knowledgeable protection of their investments. They will inevitably come to demand a more professional level of accountability from managements.

8 The Directors

> It is vain to summon a people, which has been rendered so dependent on the central power, to choose from time to time the representatives of that power; this rare and brief exercise of their free choice, however important it may be, will not prevent them from gradually losing the faculty of thinking, feeling, and acting for themselves. . . .—ALEXIS DE TOCQUEVILLE, *Democracy in America*, 1862

The board of directors *is* the agency of accountability for the corporation, and the director is in a unique legal category. He is, personally, not an agent of the corporation, since usually he does not act independently but only as a member of a group. Nor is the board an agent of the corporation, unless the law of agency is revised to permit the agent to control the principal. Also, neither the director nor the board are legal trustees, since they do not hold title to the corporation's properties and thus the essential element of trust (the *corpus* or *res*) is missing.

Like the agent and the trustee, however, the director is a fiduciary. His fiduciary duties are not easily interpreted and vary from state to state and in different corporate charters. The important basis of these duties is that they are *primarily* oriented to the corporation itself. As the California Corporation Code[1] puts it, ". . . directors and officers shall exercise their powers in good faith, and with a view to the interests of the corporation." This means that the director's fiduciary duties may be construed to conform to the demands of accountability in any of its dimensions, in keeping with the nineteenth-century model of answerability to ownership or with the complexities of the antithetical model and its social accountability.

It is generally agreed, nevertheless, that the board came to exist originally as a focal point for the exercise of the power of ownership residing in the stockholder. Does the declining vigor of the ownership role weaken this linchpin of the board's charter, or at the least, dilute or confuse the charter? And what is the effect upon the "representative democracy" analogy under which the shareholder need assume responsibility only at times of a "change in government"? It is important to gain at least a qualitative impression of the strength of the directorates of United States corporations. Outside observers, some of whom were quoted previously, take the position that the directorate is no more than an extension of the management. In fact, there is a trend in their writings to regard the two synonymously, to use the term *management* as all-inclusive and to cease referring to the directorate. Even where "outside" directors sit on a board, these observers imply that outsiders are selected by, and dependent upon, the management. Their position is that the board is not a strong organization in United States business, and the term "rubber stamp" has been generously applied.

In the view of many practicing top managers, however, the director and the board have a uniquely different function from that of management. Managers are keenly aware that those who have operating sovereignty in a corporate organization need to have their decisions reviewed in "another place," not only to illuminate or alleviate potential failures but also to validate managerial triumphs. Valuable as the management team may be, the director admittedly should not be a part of it; he should be above and beyond it, able to exercise an overview, a man of "proven probity," a pure representative of Galbraith's "lords temporal," and perhaps even possessing some of the qualities of the "lords spiritual," whose integrity sets the moral tone for their society.

There is considerable evidence that this fundamental apartness of the directorate, supported in principle by most executives in the land, is a tenet honored more in the breach than in the observance. The view of the board expressed by outside observers may be tinged with cynicism, whereas the view of the managers may be tinged with myopia. Undoubtedly strong forces at work are causing the directorate to merge with top operating management; and in this blend, apartness suffers. This tendency is rationalized by the prevalent sentiment that it is increasingly difficult to find a sufficient number of "outside" directors who measure up to the entrance requirements and who are willing to sit upon major boards.

Foresighted practicing managers are well aware that there are vast variations in strength and competency among boards in the United States. The humorous characterizations of the directorate within business are legend; frequently the board is referred to as a club for the "wise, successful, and elderly." In a session of the American Institute of Management, boards were criticized along these lines. First, there is generally no clear definition of what a board should do to carry out its job. Second, directors in general do not work hard enough at being directors. Third, too many directors are not well qualified; they are retired self-seekers or golfing friends of the chairman. Fourth, board meetings are often poorly defined, poorly planned, and poorly run.

The schism in management opinion about board functions is illustrated in these comments:

President, utility company: It is my considered opinion that about 3 per cent of the 1500 companies listed on the New York Stock Exchange have effective boards of directors. The others prostitute the function of directors—a quick once-over, rubber stamp, pick up fee and leave.

Chairman of the Board, mining company: This Board is an effective one. The management spends much time keeping it informed. The directors do their homework continually. The "outside" directors make sure that they are personally contributing. The Board sets policy in this company. It's a fine mechanism which we have spent years building.

Chairman of the Board, pharmaceutical company: The Board always goes along with the propositions of management. That's often said, and it's true. But it does not take into account the many ways in which a Board can influence these propositions before they are finally presented. Even so, if a management *insists* on its own way, the Board will always defer to it. However, if this happens, say, three of four times with adverse results, the Board will simply *change* the management. I have been on several Boards where this has happened.

Each board is a creature of its company and is tailored to that company's needs. There undoubtedly is some non-feasance to an indeterminate extent within the ranks of United States directors. But the earlier question may have been answered: Yes, declining ownership has probably also weakened the functioning of the directorates. The next question inevitably arises: How can a board be modified to permit it to be cognizant of all the obligations that the corporation owes to the society while at the same time be able to control the corporation so that it acts accordingly? This question has come up in Congress and elsewhere whenever there has been business adversity, and it will arise again repeatedly. Managements will have to add their own proviso to the question: How can a board at the same time be maintained as a positive guiding force for the economizing role of the corporation?

Many answers have been presented to the several aspects of the question. Generally the answers center about what type of board will do the best job. Chief executives of successful companies in which ownership is a potent force among the directors (for example, Crawford Greenewalt[2]) generalize about the virtues of proprietary boards, whereas critics cite case for case in which proprietary boards have ruined formerly successful companies. Officers of Standard Oil Company of New Jersey point to the impressive accomplishments of their company's classical "inside" board, but detractors cite the inherent conflicts between this type of board and the traditional and current mores of society.

Meanwhile, from government, academic, and labor sectors, regular proposals are made by advocates of two general concepts: the "public" director and the "paid" director. The former is appointed from government ranks; the latter, from the private sector. Both are of the same category, which might be labeled the "commissar" plan, an appellation used by many managers. It connotes a director who is detached from the management team and whose loyalties and interests do not coincide with those of his organization. The more adverse connotation of the "informer" with inside access is also in the term. It is not equivalent to the check-and-balance method which Americans have long adopted. It is rather analogous to a situation in which a member of the judiciary might be placed within the legislative unit to adjudicate new legislation before it is formulated or while it is being formulated. It is not hard to foresee the sharp decline of successful legislation under such a situation.

In 1940, Mr. Justice Douglas, while chairman of the Securities and Exchange Commission, advocated a system of paid directors who would constitute in effect a new profession. Speaking of the several elements of public interest in the modern corporation, Douglas noted:

One function of the paid director would be to harmonize these various elements so far as possible. For, although these elements may superficially appear to conflict, the fundamental interests of all social groups are identical over the long term. The corporate officer frequently recognizes these principles; but he is so close to his work that it is hard for him to look beyond its immediate necessities. But the paid director need not be afflicted with such nearsightedness. It would indeed be one of the defects which he would be paid not to have.[3]

Proposals for public directors on corporate boards have been made on the floor of the Congress for years, and there have been many other proposals for "paid" directors. For example, one proposal[4] emphasizes a new national association, which would be formed by all major institutional investors in the country for the purpose of appointing professional directors to the boards of all companies in which they hold large amounts of stock. These directors would be well paid by the association and would be representatives of the association.

Perhaps the most significant comment to come from the interviews for this book, significant because it was made by one of the venerable deans of investment banking in the United States, and because of the explicit meaning in his words, may be paraphrased as:

Accountability, to be effective, requires an instrument. Professional management and ownership are now fissioned, with management definitely calling the signals. Under this situation, the directorate as it is now conceived cannot be the instrument of accountability. In my view, a form of anarchy prevails.

Shareholders must secure cohesive representation because they are now one of the few unorganized groups in the society. They can do this if the banks and financial institutions will set up a group of competent directors for them, pay these directors, and see that they are seated on the boards of the major corporations. Each board would then have two or more members beholden to an outside group, and paid by them.

Thus corporate directors are regularly criticized from two points of view. One group of critics says that their outlook is not broad enough to make their corporations responsive to the needs of the society. The other group implies that their outlook is not focused enough on the matter of gaining returns for the shareholder.

The search for a new viability in a board of directors points to a new phrasing of the problem. What is really sought is a way to structure the directorate so that it simulates the accountability of the corporation. If this were achieved, then the corporation could be guided in its total economic and social roles by a board that would adjudicate the demands of the public consensus with demands for wealth-generating performance.

The board of directors, like all other institutions conceived during the age of simple ownership, has suffered in the winds of change. And the analogy that compares the shareholder to the voter, each protected by his own house of representatives, stands deeply in doubt. The directorate has a crucial function in accountability, but its function has not been fully defined.

PART III

But rational, systematic, and specialized pursuit of
science, with trained and specialized personnel, has
only existed in the West in a sense at all approaching
its present dominant place in our culture. Above all
is this true of the trained official, the pillar of
both the modern State and of the economic life of the
West. He forms a type of which there have heretofore
only been suggestions, which have never remotely
approached its present importance for the social order.

—MAX WEBER, in
  *The Protestant Ethic and the
  Spirit of Capitalism,* 1930

9 Management: End of the Empiric Era

> To idealize the professional spirit would be very absurd; it has its sordid side, and, if it is to be fostered in industry, safeguards will be needed to check its excesses. But there is all the difference between maintaining a standard which is occasionally abandoned, and affirming as the central truth of existence that there is no standard to maintain.—R. H. TAWNEY in *The Acquisitive Society*, 1920

In 1793, when the institution of medicine was in the middle of its empiric age, the city of Philadelphia lay in the grip of a yellow fever epidemic. One of the great physicians in medical history, Dr. Benjamin Rush, was called into consultation. His empirical analysis led him to conclude that the disease resulted from an "oppressed state of the system," and he prescribed bleeding and purging. Remarkably, the first four patients so treated all recovered, and subsequently the same severe treatment was repeatedly prescribed by his disciples. It would be impossible to determine how many human lives were sacrificed to this "conclusive" demonstration.

A student of the medical occupation,[1] writing in 1912, noted the "amazing assurance" exhibited by practitioners as they prescribed a severe medication based upon an unfounded diagnosis. It was further noted that although medical dogma had been repressed, passionate and emotional arguments were still used to demonstrate to students the "truth" of a particular concept.

The institution of medicine almost floundered in its late empiric era, even with its relative advances in knowledge, and in spite of the great names it had produced: Rush, Hahnemann, Osler, and others. *Its practitioners, individually and collectively, could not provide the services and the competency that the public consensus demanded.* Although a few great doctors with unique personal resources prevailed against the institutional inadequacies, there were far too many lesser men whose competency was subprofessional. Commencing about 1910, medicine engaged in an arduous bootstrap operation, which enabled it to resurrect its accountability to the public, provide for its survival, and expand its horizons to an increasing tempo of achievement. The purpose of this operation was to establish a medical profession, and the purpose was achieved.

Management's empiric era has produced great accomplishments, and management has had its own great names. But in the recent past, there have been implications that the public is demanding a general higher level of performance, and there has been the disturbing loss of understanding with regard to accountability, as reported in earlier chapters. There are also increasing signs that the overuse of dogma in the discussion of economic and social issues, whether from management or any other institution, is wearing thin in the public consensus. Witness Sylvia Porter's recent comment:

The rigid clinging to obsolete points of view and the ignorance of today's economic realities disclosed at the White House Conference on National Economic Issues . . . by many of the top labor and business leaders of this nation are frightening to any informed observer. . . .

It was the same old stuff—labor leaders calling for higher

wages, businessmen calling for higher profits, "public" representatives calling for lower prices—and scarcely anyone digging beneath the superficialities and down to the basic solutions to the problems. . . .[2]

A. H. Raskin,[3] writing in *The Reporter*, spoke of the "barrenness of ideas in management, labor, and the academic community" on economic matters. And Secretary of the Treasury Dillon, in an address in 1962 urged that:

. . . the confusion of myth and reality, of fact with fiction, when considering the complex problems of the day, is not in our national interest. . . .

Every intelligent United States manager knows that he has his own "dogma point," a point at which dogma and ideology come boiling to the surface. He may criticize government intervention in a certain problem while remaining unwilling to participate in the solution of that problem by nongovernmental means. He may denounce the expanding functions of government while promoting government activity beneficial to his own sphere of business. He may argue against economic planning in the macrosphere while promoting corporate economic planning to the ultimate in his own microsphere, and be troubled by lack of a clear rationale for this schism. Any manager can provide a list of issues upon which his present position is frozen, unresolved, in a state of strained logic; and indeed Clarence Randall, in his book *The Folklore of Management*, not long ago published an insightful collection of managerial "myths" prevailing in modern corporate enterprise.

In our economic society the public is fully aware that it needs the benefits of effective economic organizations and competent administration within them, be they large or small. This predilection for the moderate approach and the economic philosophy of the middle class thrusts management into the key economic role. The manager can be the guiding force, if he can assume the challenge.

The public will further demand that managerial guidance be effectively accountable in its use of economic and human resources and that this accountability be demonstrable. At the same time, the public will call for the end of superficiality, emotion, dogma, and ideology—all plainly offered to disguise lack of depth and knowledge—from whatever quarter in the discussion of socio-economic problems. In short, the public is fed up with dogma and heat where rationality and light are needed. If the age of ideology is fast fading, as scholars insist,[4] then management must be among the recognizers of the fact.

Another force that augurs the end of empirical management is the essential toughness of the competitive economic environment in the 1960s—an environment that will demand the most competent men in the manager corps. The bland 1950s offered a general shortage of consumer goods, a short supply of labor, a lack of sufficient industrial production capacity, a lack of real industrial competition from foreign sources, and a favorable balance of international payments. None of these fine conditions will prevail in the years immediately ahead, and only a fully established profession of management can provide the precise guidance required.

Managers are weary of exercising their half-knowledge. They are hungry for a professional's blend of experience and theory, which will allow them, first, to know when they are on the firm ground of present knowledge in operating their enterprises, and second, to evaluate accurately the degree of risk they assume when they must venture away from firm ground. They want sufficient knowledge, experience, and dedication to permit them to suppress dogmatic argument, to relieve the strained logic, and cut away the "myths" which make management's present position increasingly uncomfortable. They will gain their goals when they achieve the status and responsibilities of a fully professional institution of management.

The Elements of a Profession

> Comparative study of the social structures of the most important civilizations shows that the professions occupy a position of importance in our society which is, in any comparable degree of development, unique in history.—TALCOTT PARSONS in *Essays in Sociological Theory, Pure and Applied,* 1949.

Men have long argued about the relative merits of the judgment of the people, the "public consensus," versus the judgment of the trained peer groups in the smaller organizations of society. Centuries before the form of modern professions began to emerge, Aristotle discoursed in *The Politics* upon this topic, implying that the judgment of the peers might be the more informed and practical, and noting that in all the professions and arts, this rule should apply:

As, then, the physician ought to be called to account by physicians, so ought men in general to be called to account by their peers.

Conversely, Aristotle then observed that the judgment of the multitude might in some manner yield the better answers:

... if the people are not utterly degraded, although individually they may be worse judges than those who have special knowledge—as a body they are as good or better. ...

The professions were created as one way to resolve this long conflict in democratic political thought, which compares the competency of the peer as judge against the truth-finding ability and humanitarian goodness of the multitude as judge. The objective is to have the best of both worlds—to allow the professional to be accountable to his equals in achievement within the microsphere, and yet to require each professional group to be accountable to society. The structure of accountability is designed, imposed, and maintained by the group itself, but explicitly demonstrable to society and understood within society. As discussed earlier, Toynbee and other scholars have persuasively argued that when responsibility becomes a personal trait voluntarily exercised, the result is that enterprise, innovation, and achievement thrive. Where responsibility is enforced from outside the group, the results are opposite.

Since the 1920s, sociologists have been analyzing the professions in an effort to isolate the traits that distinguish a professional man in the Western occupational structures. Two items emerge as *core traits* in establishing professional standing.[5] The first is the "common body of knowledge," a requirement for prolonged specialized training of all members in an abstract body of knowledge. The second is a collective and individual orientation to the concept of public service, with an implied element of disinterestedness connected with the rendering of service. Further implied in this second general trait is the existence of a set of ethics to govern the practice of the profession and to maintain a high level of public service.

A third key element of a profession is an active *practice* on the part of all members, which is the focal point where experience and theory are interwoven by the skillful practitioner. Candidates for the profession must always learn by doing, by performing experimental work, and must not merely acquire passively from lecture or book. Other important elements have been identified.[6] A dominant element is rationalism—the seeking out of the new and the best—as opposed to traditionalism. Another factor is universalism, the previously discussed concept, which insists that *who* states a proposition within the profession is irrelevant to the technical merits of the proposition. Thus universality focuses upon technical competency and discourages personal associations and cliques that might becloud objectivity.

The remaining key elements of a profession have to do with the *dedication* and the *authority* of its members. The practice of the professional group must be dedicated to a high purpose. In principle, the commitment of attorneys collectively to the law and of physicians collectively to the protection of the public health are examples of dedication that goes beyond the immediate day-to-day commitment to each case as it comes. Authority in the professions is related to the ancient Roman magisterium, or teaching office, and may be defined as a quality that deserves deference because of the knowledge of the holder. It is opposite to the concept of *power* in its coercive, juridical dimensions. Authority in the professions is marked by a restriction the sociologists call "specificity of knowledge"; a professional person is scrupulous to exercise his authority only in the fields of knowledge in which he is explicitly qualified.

From these key elements, the analysts have gone on to define lesser elements, which are sociologically derivative rather than causative. Some of these[7] are:

1. The profession determines its own standards for education and training.

2. The student professional goes through a much more extensive adult indoctrination procedure than does the learner in an occupation.

3. Professional practice is often but not always legally recognized by some form of licensing.

4. Most of the legislation concerning the profession is shaped by it, as long as the profession maintains its public acceptance.

5. When an occupation becomes a profession, its members gain in income, power, and prestige in the community. Significantly, the profession can always attract the young candidates of higher caliber.

6. Practitioners of the profession are relatively free from lay evalution and control.

7. The norms of practice enforced by the profession are more stringent than any legislative controls or other externally imposed controls.

8. Members are more strongly identified and affiliated with the profession than are members of an occupational group.

9. The profession is more likely to be a terminal kind of work for members. In general, members do not care to leave it, and a high proportion indicate that they would enter the same field if the chance were provided to start over again.

The institution of management may be evaluated in terms of these criteria, to determine the outlook for converting an incipient professional status to an established one, and to weigh the prospects for instilling a professional accountability in the practitioners and for gaining acceptance by the public. The first requirement, a common body of knowledge, is controversial when applied to management. Certainly management knowledge does not consist of the so-called hard sciences in which truth is identifiable only by experiment, as in the physical sciences. However, law is not a hard science, yet it is an established profession. It is also true that management is a generalized technique rather than a specialized one, and it is thereby difficult to limit the scope of the underlying knowledge. Here again, however, the older professions have also tended to branch out into an increasing number of specialties, resulting in a continuously broadening scope of underlying knowledge.

Strong forces are at work to build the common body of

management knowledge. These are the graduate business schools, the management associations, and the various management consulting organizations. The few good graduate schools, via the continual improvement of their curricula, are powerfully shaping the structure of management knowledge. Similarly, management associations, in their conferences and seminars, are extending the boundaries of management learning.[8] The professional management-consulting organizations have built up massive files of case work, which contain a wealth of management knowledge.

One who has observed any modern profession at work will intuitively conclude that although sociologists are basically correct in their emphasis upon the common body of knowledge, there is room for at least two important qualifications. First, where a common knowledge is difficult to define, it can be replaced by a carefully developed common sense of responsibility.[9] In medicine, a psychiatrist and an orthopedic surgeon at one stage in their learning share a common knowledge of the prerequisites in general medicine, but in later phases of their careers, it is much more likely that they share a strong sense of common responsibility, while each progresses in a broad field of knowledge that is not familiar to the other.

The second qualification is that modern professions are staffed by those who are capable of competent practice and who utilize to a varying extent the underlying body of knowledge. Thus members of a profession hold in common a set of abilities, which enable them to practice successfully, and abilities are a better measure of the professional than is knowledge. Many efforts have been made to categorize the essential abilities of a competent manager.[10] One of the most succinct statements of the required abilities of the management practitioner was made by Lawrence Appley, president of the American Management Association, in an address before the International Management Congress at Brussels in 1951. Appley said that the manager must be able to:

1. Maintain the economic health of an organization.

2. Integrate the viewpoints of different management functions and people within it.

3. Direct the affairs of an organization in proper relationship to the community, the industry, the national, and international economies.

4. Instill a service motive into the organization which takes into account the incommensurables—loyalty, tradition, friendship, understanding, courage, patience, perseverance, and spiritual values.

5. Make an organization dynamic, adaptable to changes.

6. Provide human satisfaction in work output and relationships.

Each of these general abilities is now reasonably well accepted throughout the management institution as a requisite for satisfactory management performance in widely varying lines of industrial endeavor. Moreover, each required ability is also a responsibility, and a deep conviction is developing within management that it must begin to insist upon the proper discharge of these responsibilities throughout the American corporate sector. During several conflict-of-interest cases, which plagued business in 1959 and 1960 in such diverse industries as automobiles and insurance, there was a considerable amount of disapproval generated in executive offices and board rooms across the land. Management is at the point of incipient peer enforcement, which will be inconspicuously exercised (as in all professions) but effective.

Common responsibility leads directly to the second core trait that identifies a profession; that is, the collectivity devoted to public service and the associated concept of disinterestedness in personal gain. (To illustrate: The insti-

tution of medicine is expected to provide service for its
indigent customers regardless of the probability of being
paid.) Social scientists have paid particular attention to the
elements of *service* and *altruism* in the professions, chiefly
because it is "the pursuit of self-interest" elucidated by
Adam Smith so many years ago which is often alleged to
separate management forever from the professions.

If "altruistic" types of institutions prosper notably along
with the "egoistic" institution of business in our society, then
what are the true differences in motivation between the
practitioners in the two institutions? Talcott Parsons[11] considered the goals of ambition for individuals within each
type of institution and found them to be essentially the same.
Each group in reality defines success as (1) the satisfactory
attainment of the technical goals of the specialty, and
(2) attainment of high standing or recognition in the peer
group.

In management or in the established professions, achievement must lead to commensurate recognition if the institution is to establish effective sanctions for desirable
performance. Deviant behavior, such as an outbreak of shady
practice in the law, is believed to be a reaction to the strains
resulting when this articulation breaks down. Sociologists
have concluded reasonably that there is no difference between the typical *personal motivations* of a manager and a
doctor or lawyer. But there have always been clear differences between the professions and the occupations in the *institutional level* of public service that is expected. For many
years management has continuously shifted its position
with regard to service to the public, and has also modified
its concepts of *how much* and *in what manner* the practitioner may reap personal tangible rewards. At some point
in this process, management reaches a position where its
collective standards of public service and personal disinter-

estedness are on the same plane as those of the established profession. It is academic to speculate whether this position was attained in 1950, or in 1960, or will be attained in 1970. The important element is the near approach.

Management as a profession will have to face squarely, and resolve, one of the thorniest questions about the economic scene. How much compensation should managers withdraw from corporations? In framing this answer, managers may harken to the shrewd limits imposed by Aristotle when he spoke of the good fortune of a state where the citizens have a *moderate* and *sufficient* property. They may remember the Ethic, which held that acquisitiveness must be bounded, and note that it always was bounded by most of the entrepreneurs who built the market society. It was fundamental to capitalism that the man (or state) who would industrialize or reindustrialize must first deprive himself of consumption. And they should be constrained by the essence of modern professional ethics, which holds that a professional must receive his basic satisfaction from professional achievement and only secondary satisfaction from what his work produces materially. Finally, managers know that many of the men in the executive offices today do receive their most important rewards in achievement; it is a declining few who persist in taking disproportionate benefits from the corporate largesse, as Clarence Randall points out in *The Folklore of Management*.[12]

When many professionals practice actively within the corporation (physicists, chemists, doctors, lawyers, economists, psychologists), the limits of the various authorities of knowledge become a crucial problem. Management has deliberately sought to understand better its own authority of knowledge and to clarify the relationship between this authority and that of the contributing professionals by fostering study in the behavioral sciences and by clinical experiments in industry. In the aerospace industries, as an illustration, an observer of a conference between a department manager and a chief aerodynamicist would be struck by the similarity to the typical unctuous relationship between a physician and a dental surgeon examining a patient whose injury unhappily belongs partially in both their domains.

In many of their decisions, managers continue to exercise power, in its coercive sense, originating in hierarchal position, as opposed to the authority of knowledge. Many managers have long realized what the organizational scientists now confirm; that is, that the condition where maximum authority is utilized is the condition of maximum freedom for accomplishment within the organization. Yet they also understand that where the occasion is appropriate, *power* must be exercised to maintain an organizational action toward established goals. In no way does this use of power disqualify management from professional status any more than does its use by the doctor who is the chief administrator of a hospital or the lawyer who is dean of a university law school. Within the concept of specific authority, there is again no apparent ground upon which management may be differentiated from the older professions.

When management becomes professional, there will be those who want to license or certify it. Generally the men of management believe that this will be a mistake, and they support their position in this way:

True, the advancement of medicine has been enhanced since its licensing requirement was instituted. But this illustrates the point. We have within business many individual contributors who are professionals. By all means, let them continue to be certified to practice, the more rigorously the better. Let the engineers and the lawyers go to the legislature regularly to tighten the registration and admission requirements. This will not stultify their fields; rather it will advance them and strengthen them as long as they don't overdo it.

But in management the practice is much broader and the situation is totally different. First, certification would let all the legislatures in. It would become a matter of survival to our society that the boundaries be wisely defined, that is, where and when does a man have to go before a board, meet requirements defined by local laws, before he can enter into management? We are not wise enough to resolve these questions appropriately.

In lieu of seeking certification or license, managers feel that they must hew to the real task of building a viable profession. The task cannot be expressed more cogently than Vannevar Bush has put it:

It is by no means fully recognized that the profession of management exists. For those who believe in our system and who would perpetuate it, there is no more rewarding effort than to see that this recognition becomes general and real. This does not mean organization or propaganda. It means in essence that the professional attitude shall become enhanced and emphasized wherever men of business gather. It means especially that the neophytes, entering the long ladder which leads to great responsibilities, become early inculcated with the professional spirit, as they see it exercised by those above them on the climb. It means, above all, that there shall be an increasing solidarity among members of the profession, not in formal ways, but in those subtle influences which are exceedingly powerful, in the growth of mutual understanding, in willingness to talk frankly in a professional way, in an exclusiveness not formally defined, but understandable, which makes it clear that true membership in the professional group is highly desirable, and to be obtained only by living the life of a professional man and securing the accolade of those who thus live.[13]

Whether or not management has crossed the amorphous boundary into the territory of a profession, corporate administration is now a vocation that can be professionally defined, professionally approached, and professionally staffed. Within this vocation, men who view their work as a profession are increasingly sought, and the steady building of professional standards goes on.

Most important, management practitioners are learning that their work, as is any profession, is a unique combination of science and art. Where science governs their practice, managers will utilize the cold objectivity of science; where art governs, managers will understand what they do not yet know, and act accordingly, with appropriate deference to the unknown.

In taking the final steps in this great transformation, managers will escape the strains and bury the myths that have burdened their recent existence. They will be trading these for the more rigorous but more rewarding demands of the true professional role. They will be accepting the challenge to construct, establish, and maintain their own accountability to their society.

10 The Third Culture

What is really needed today is not exclusivity of knowledge, but a deeper unity of all knowledge, past, present, and yet to come.—THE REV. THEODORE M. HESBURGH, president of the University of Notre Dame, in a commencement address at M.I.T.

Industrial managers must be accountable for their use of both the *economic* resources of society and the *human* resources of society. Contemporary corporate management has been criticized for the alleged erosion of accountability in these essential dimensions. Therefore it is reasonable to conclude that management will first have to establish its professional relationships with those men who probe the basic material nature of our world; second, and perhaps more importantly, with those who probe to understand man in the universe.

In recent years much has been said about two cultures. The first is the culture of those who work with abstractions in the humanities, the liberal arts and the fine arts, and who thereby understand man, his aspirations, and his deficiencies; the second, quite unlinked with the first, is the culture of those who work with the pure and applied sciences and who thereby understand the world of things.[1]

Management as a profession must find its place in the sun. It is fair to suspect that there are more than two basic cul-

tures, and the world of the modern professions may constitute a third culture. In its essence, a modern profession is,
after all, a sophisticated merger of science and art. In expanding this hypothesis, the unique features of the management profession should be considered. First, in common
with the inhabitants of the first culture (literary intellectuals, artists, educators in the arts, political statesmen, and
opinion formers generally), managers use words, abstractions, and concepts in the practice of their emerging disciplines. Moreover, management has been thrust into the role
of governance of the efforts of men in ever larger organizations, and managers henceforth cannot avoid increasing
pressures to understand men and mankind. Thus there may
be, at the least, a basis for mutual understanding between
professional managers and the first culture, a culture nour-
ished by very learned men whose understanding of the
nature of our material cosmos is limited and whose most
complex tool of work is generally the typewriter.

However, in contrast to these other utilizers of abstractions, management bears an explicit interest in the tangible
results of what it says and does. That is, management is
committed to productivity, which is measurable, and thereby
to comprehensive understanding *and* utilization of the detailed principles, ever-changing techniques, and complex
machinery of the total physical environment of the economy.
Managers, in their day-to-day routine, are accustomed to
merging the outputs of practitioners of the "hard" sciences
(that is, solid-state physics) with the outputs of men versed
in the "soft" sciences (such as industrial psychology)
and then further synthesizing the work of these specialists with the governance of productive men and the use
of arrays of complex production machinery. Professional
management is potentially and uniquely in a position to
bridge the gap of understanding between those who use the

processes of the mind to understand man's history and destiny and those who use the mind to understand nature and exploit it for the immediate purposes of man.

During the score of years since business and industry have made use of subatomic particles, and since the scientific revolution has been felt in full impact within the economy, managers have gained a generation of experience in how they should work with the professional technologist. True, the path toward accord has been rough, and there have been obstructions and blind alleys, all of which have been analyzed in the segment of the management literature devoted to the "scientific mind" and the "management mind." Nevertheless, there has been real progress. The emergence of a management profession can do much to strengthen this young relationship and enhance the communication between the manager and the scientist or engineer.[2] However, the crucial relationship of management to the liberal intellectual—a relation staged in the whole arena of society and not within corporations alone—is yet to be determined.

If the profession of management would be prepared to participate in the third culture, the crucial middle ground between the arts and the sciences, then management needs to scrutinize closely the educational processes that produce managerial candidates.

Education of Managers

> . . . and studies themselves do give forth directions too much at large, except they be bounded in by experience.—
> FRANCIS BACON, *Essays*, 1625

A profession is established and maintained by the total educational program that it requires its members to complete, including both its formal preprofessional academic process and also the subsequent training pressures, which the sociologists call the "adult indoctrination process."

In recent years there have been major studies of American business education. The Ford Foundation financed the 1959 study by R. A. Gordon of the University of California and J. E. Howell of Stanford, entitled *Higher Education for Business*. The Carnegie Corporation of New York commissioned the 1959 report by Frank C. Pierson of Swarthmore College, entitled *The Education of American Businessmen: A Study of University-College Programs in Business Administration*.

These reports were sharp indictments of the condition of business education in America. Just as in 1900 there were at best perhaps one-half dozen medical schools where the faculty was devoted to a professional conviction of medicine, so these reports imply that there were about that many professionally oriented management schools in 1959. The investigators found that, in general, and with the exception of only a few of the graduate schools, the academic standards of America's 160 schools of business[3] were much too low. Particularly in the undergraduate business schools and in the business administration departments, the curricula suffered from lack of coherence and were deficient in analytical content. As a result of the low standards[4] "many students who do not have either the background or the innate ability to survive a rigorous college program are admitted to the business schools."

Further, the teaching methods in most of these schools were inadequate and deteriorating. There was a tendency to stress passive learning methods by the student in lieu of active participation. With the single exception of the subject of accounting, business students in the 1950s were given little or no opportunity to engage in laboratory work or to undertake independent analysis. Mostly they listened to exposition by the instructor. The reports generalized that most business school faculties suffered from[5] "creeping intellectual obsolescence," and they highlighted the widespread lack of a stimulating intellectual atmosphere in these institutions. In particular, the investigators noted the disappointing output of significant research or new knowledge from the faculties.

It is the official "position" of the American Association of Collegiate Schools of Business that at least 40 per cent of the total hours required for a bachelor's degree should be taken in subjects other than business, that is, in science and the liberal arts. The Pierson study concluded that in 1959 this position was noteworthy only in its near-universal violation in the schools. In other words, science and the liberal arts were unduly neglected, and the average business student learned for the most part "techniques" in business subjects. In 1959 one American business college offered 188 undergraduate courses, and many others offered more than 100. Each of the core subjects, such as finance, production, or accounting, had been continuously broken down into subspecialties.

A more fundamental problem underlies contemporary business education. It may be roughly estimated that in all American companies of more than 100 employees, only about 100,000 persons can by any definition be considered members of top management, and in the large corporations, considerably fewer. Yet the business units of American colleges and universities are turning out 50,000 graduates in business administration each year. There were actually more than one-half million of these graduates in business during the decade 1948–1958.[6]

These figures mean that only a negligible percentage of the country's business graduates can hope to assume truly professional management positions. The utilization of such a proportion of American student resources, and such a proportion of its educational resources, to turn out these graduates becomes a crucial question for education and for the public; it is also a question that demands some positive attention from American management. What is the justification for continuing to turn out large numbers of poor students, by poor methods, taught by poor faculties, who face poor prospects after graduation? More basically, what is a "business" manager? Is there any discernible similarity between a manager's function in a large, multidivision industrial corporation and the manager's function in a bowling alley or a retail store? If comparable numbers of students continue to insist upon a business education, what type of education should it be? If the majority of them will assume relatively low-level positions in industry or will take over their fathers' small businesses, what is their most appropriate curriculum?

Most importantly for a management profession, what is the long-term effect of these large numbers of graduates with mediocre training, year after year, upon the public's conception of management and business?

The 1959 studies recommend that academic standards in the business schools be "materially" raised and should in fact be *higher* than for the college population in general, as they are in any other profession. Business schools must sharply advance their entrance requirements, quit their role as a refuge for college rejects. "Students who cannot do college level work do not belong in college." Then the business curricula must be shorn of vocationalism and overspecialization, must be bolstered in the liberal arts and sciences and in broader courses in policy, principles, and theory. There should be a two-year graduate program, with a professional rather than academic orientation. Doctoral programs must be expanded and improved, and the quality of business research must be improved.

The task is large. Managerial candidates have to be exposed, in the sum of their undergraduate and post-graduate training, to much background in the humanities and in the behavioral sciences and a broad spectrum of the physical sciences. They must as well be drilled in the specific disciplines of corporate business in a capitalist system of enterprise—fundamentals such as corporate finance and control. In addition, a manager at some point must assimilate the rudiments of macroeconomic analysis. The term *exposed* was used above deliberately because the members of modern professions cannot hope to encompass in their knowledge all the specialties supporting their practice. Consider medicine; the general practitioner cannot be expert in bacteriology, pharmacology, histology, or any of several other key disciplines. Yet he must have a proper appreciation of all, based upon sufficient acquired knowledge in each field.

On the international management scene, the present picture is still pessimistic. The recent CIOS-Ford Foundation Study concluded that intuitive and dogmatic management (as opposed to a professional approach) still heavily dominates the entire management institution abroad. Overseas, there is still great reliance on the traditional power of ownership, applied bluntly and independently of qualification. A good manager is hard to find. Out of 85 million estimated managers (business and all other categories) in the world, only about 6 million, or 7 per cent, participate in the worldwide management improvement movement. And perhaps 10 million would qualify as knowledgeable, by rudimentary professional standards. The report notes a common "illusion" in many nations, which pictured a nation's own managers as exceptional improvisors, capable of solving tough managerial problems intuitively through their supernormal judgment and experience. All in all, this report supports a conclusion that, *on a world-wide basis*, the emergence of an active profession founded upon both practice and learning and with a clear relationship to underlying sciences and liberal arts, is only beginning.

In the medical world of fifty years ago, the first crucial step toward basic improvement was the cleaning up of a mess in the majority of the so-called medical schools of the day. *Educational deficiencies are impassable stumbling blocks in the pathway to professional status.* The manner in which comprehensive recommendations of recent studies are put into effect is crucial to the future of management.

It is reassuring to observe that business educators and managements have responded constructively to recent criticisms. As of 1963, more graduate management schools with professional curricula are being established, and a growing number of undergraduate business schools with subprofessional standards is being discontinued. Faculties are being upgraded, and entrance requirements are becoming more stringent. The trend toward fragmentation of curricula has been stopped. Over-all, a more positive picture of management education begins to emerge in the 1960s.

Managers, Values, and Intellectuals

> Civilization has had to await the beginning of the twentieth century to see the astounding spectacle of how brutal, how stupid, and yet how aggressive is the man learned in one thing and fundamentally ignorant of all else. Professionalism and specialism, through insufficient counterbalancing, have smashed the European man in pieces.—JOSE ORTEGA Y GASSETT in *The Mission of the University,* 1933

In Germany in the 1930s and early 1940s, there were many splendidly performing industrial corporations in which the managers were accountable to, and attuned with, the aims of the society. In 1944, one of these managers sent a letter to Gestapo headquarters in Berlin in which he wrote:

We suggest two crematoria furnaces for the building planned, but we advise you to make further inquiries to make sure that two ovens will be sufficient for your requirements.

We guarantee the effectiveness of the cremation ovens as well as their durability, the use of the best material and our faultless workmanship.[7]

The letter was from a company that had previously furnished ovens for Dachau and Lublin, and was signed in the custom of the day, "Heil Hitler!"

Here, "faultless workmanship" is an illustration of a traditional dilemma for the professional, which will become a towering problem for the profession of management. Professional persons stand with one foot in the sciences and the other in the arts. They can fall prey to the excess inherent in either camp—the abused amorality of science or the unlicensed and uncalibrated preoccupation with value-formation practiced by some exponents of the liberal and fine arts.

Since the time of Newton, the physical scientist has tended to operate in a value vacuum. His successes have been glamorous, and as much as any other force he has led the world away from the religious-scholastic school (which was preoccupied with values and in which true knowledge was believed to come only by process of mental reflections) to the scientific school, which is amoral and in which knowledge can come only via sensory perception of experimental results. Webster defines amoral as meaning "outside the sphere in which moral distinctions or judgments apply."

Thus the men of science, who have built one of the two cultures, are inclined to ignore values as a result of years of rigorous scientific methodology. Abuse and evil can spring from this methodology; yet it is naive for the public not to understand the place and the need for amorality within the practice of true scientific investigation. Similarly, abuse and evil are always latent in the work of those commentators and writers of the other culture, who would sway and mold the public consensus, who would find their way to that which is true and good by unsupported thought processes. Nevertheless there is vital need for guardians of the public conscience.

The traditional guardian of the Western conscience has been the church, and Western businessmen have turned increasingly in recent years to the churches to aid them in understanding the relationship between Christian values and the economic function.[8] We are witnessing determined efforts by the theologian and the industrial manager to understand each other, along with an increasing amount of discussion of moral issues within management circles. Secretary of Commerce Hodges says, "I believe that a great moral debate is well under way in American business."[9]

It will be a principal duty of the profession of management to ensure that these discussions and debates are applicable to the real problem of morality in management, and in this effort it should find the theologians, in most cases, cooperative partners. The real problem is one easy to oversimplify. The comments of businessmen interviewed in a 1959 survey[10] by a Catholic layman are representative of comments often heard within management:

When I need moral guidance, the last place I would go for it is the church.

If I took the advice of the clergy, I would either be out of business in a month or be involved in twice as many moral perplexities as I started out with.

Or consider the opposite oversimplification. In 1946 one common statement entitled, *Pattern for Economic Justice, A Catholic, Jewish and Protestant Declaration*,[11] set forth eight general principles constructed chiefly by theologians for observance by those working within the companies. Two of these principles are stated:

The moral law must govern economic life.
The profit motive must be subordinated to the moral law.

These principles are general and they may represent truth of the highest order, but they miss the important points: How are they to be applied within the corporate microspheres of society, and what other general truths may also require application in the microspheres? A specific task for the management profession will be to provide ethical and practical ways to answer these questions *at the work place*.

For, there is a place for amorality in its highest sense within the scientific components of a profession; there is some defensible truth in the cliches of two professions: "Business is business," and "Justice is blind." If a modern corporation becomes threatened with economic extinction, for whatever reason, its managers now have scientific tools that can indicate corrective action. In manufacturing, marketing, and accounting, vast amounts of data can be processed and reduced to the point where action is implied. It is not necessarily true that scientifically approached decisions that will be best for the corporation's survival will be simply moral in a Judaeo-Christian sense for the human welfare of its employees. The survival of this one economic entity, with all that it may imply for the good of society, must be balanced against the dislocating and sometimes cruel effects of drastic remedial actions upon employees and communities.

The decision maker must be a professional, practicing in a profession that has wisely integrated moral order into its structure of ethics and its practice. He must be a decision maker who has undergirded his professional sophistication with a philosophy toward mankind that fits the mores of his society. And similarly, the churchman must expand his understanding. In the words of the National Council of Churches:

> The Church recognizes that . . . many essential elements should be blended in judgments that the Church or its members make about economic issues. . . . Thus no one of these requisites can be omitted: Christian objectives, standards, and attitudes; technical knowledge; seasoned judgment based upon actual participation in economic activities; and awareness of the human effect of any policy upon all groups of people as those groups themselves see it.[12]

As the management profession collectively begins to understand how it must establish values within its practices, it will come to face a related problem. In a pluralistic society, all professional groups have to decide how much they should and can influence the policies of other groups and the policies of the large power centers, including the federal government. An extreme example will illustrate the point: If industry is an instrument of the national purpose, and the national purpose becomes totalitarian, what should be the role of the industrialist? As the industrialist becomes a non-owning professional manager, as he codifies his ethics, the question becomes more difficult to answer.

The modern professional will have to chart his course between two polar principles when he considers the public's influencing of values. On the one hand, there is the traditional American freedom of any citizen to indulge in factionalism, to express himself openly on the issues that determine the national position, irrespective of how well prepared or endowed he may be to make the expression. On the other hand, there is the traditional professional limitation of specificity of authority, which prohibits a professional from asserting himself in areas where he is not explicitly qualified. Abuse of the former privilege breeds political irresponsibility in which a citizen defaults in one of his basic obligations in a democratic society—his obligation to know the rudiments of what he is talking about. Overly rigorous adherence to the latter principle leads to continuously narrowing horizons, and eventually to nearly complete amorality like that of the professional physicist who will wield his specialty for any ideology because he does not "know" about values.

The professional manager of industry will find little to attract him in either of these extremes. Management cannot affect the pose of the specialist who does not care what happens in society beyond the confines of his narrow vision. The corollary is that management will thereby find occasions when it cannot avoid speaking publicly, and will have to endure the spotlight turned upon those who address the public consensus. In this case, as Clarence Randall says, ". . . if the executive cannot write his own speech, let him make none . . . let him be himself at all times."[13]

In the other direction, management should avoid factional or dogmatic positions and also the superficialities of the promotional or "public relations" approach to professional problems. A profession performs, demonstrates, and persuades by reason. It does not promote.

PART IV

An economy should be judged by what it adds
to the wealth of a nation, and to the wealth of
nations. Beyond that goal, judgment should
measure its effect on men, on politics, and
on the values and culture of the society.

—EUGENE V. ROSTOW
Planning for Freedom, 1959

11 The Real Problem

If one studies a factory, an army group, or other large organization, one wonders how things get done at all, with the lack of leadership and with all the featherbedding. Perhaps they get done because we are still trading on our reserves of inner-direction, especially in the lower ranks. At any rate, the fact they do get done is no proof that there is someone in charge.—DAVID RIESMAN in *The Lonely Crowd,* 1950

Since the founding days of the United States, the nation's citizens have been preoccupied with the *form* of the political safeguards that protect life, liberty, and the pursuit of happiness. Now they want to know not only that the corporate sector has not usurped unchecked power in the society, but also what means are in existence to prevent this from happening.

The problem of the corporation in its environment is compounded by American traits. Americans have long shown a willingness to lease large concentrations of economic power to the corporations because they recognize that concentration is needed to produce, supply, and distribute goods and services. But this power is not given irrevocably, and it must be checked by demonstrable and understood means. And Americans are intractable in their concern about grants of power over human beings.[1] For this reason, the previously cited criticisms of corporate use of this type of power will find receptive public opinion.

The problem of accountability is spotlighted in the weakness of the present link between the intracorporate and extracorporate environments. There is a well-known gulf between public policy (and public behavior via the instrument of government) on the one hand, and corporate policy and business behavior on the other. This gulf has not been bridged by the political scientist, the economist, or the manager. Of these, only the economist has tried, and in this attempt, he has failed singularly. The dean of a prominent graduate management school expressed himself on this subject:

> We can't succeed in understanding the corporation in its environment in terms of three-hundred-year-old political theory from Locke, or later theory from Jefferson; or in terms of one-hundred-and-fifty-year-old classical economic theory. These offer a good foundation, give us some insights, but someone has to build a modern superstructure over them. The theories of the firm set forth in modern economics don't begin to shed any light on the way a modern corporation operates, or should operate.[2]

At the time when economics first emerged as a discipline, its fundamental theory was that of a proprietor operating his firm in his own self-interest. Shortly thereafter, the unfortunate term *profit maximizing* must have been adopted. Later generations of economists have not restrained their inclination to expand the original meaning of the term and use it to account for all human motivation in industry. But the complex drives, objectives, and actions of modern managerial man lead him to reject such a blanket translation of business and industrial purpose. As the impacts of his decisions radiate throughout his society, he must push his horizons farther and farther into the future. The simplifying camouflage of the over-all profit motive distracts him and distorts the true import of his decisions. Managers have had always to contend with this bogey, but their resistance has been ineffective. Now some economists have begun to understand the manager's viewpoint and their barbs have penetrated the thinking of their colleagues. L. H. Jenks writes:

Economists . . . have commonly operated with loose, casual, antiquated, and inconsistent assumptions about human behavior.[3]

Several years ago, at an annual meeting of the American Economic Association, the eminent economist Charles Lindblom questioned the narrow approach of his profession in the interpretation of the corporation. He noted a long line of "provocative" essays and books from other disciplines that had analyzed the corporation but had failed to divert economists from their habit of treating the corporation simply as a profit-maximizing individual. He concluded:

. . . it is no doubt true that if we as economists were to take account of the many dimensions of the corporation in our theory, we would take on a very great burden. It would mean that we would lose some of our professional distinctiveness and that we would become social scientists with specialization in economics rather than economists.[4]

The economist understands and makes essential contributions in macroeconomics—national income determination, monetary and fiscal policies, and allied subjects—whereas the manager is oriented to the environment within the corporation. They each use the same terms—price, market, competition, among others—not realizing that they intend different meanings. They do not understand each other's problems, yet the reflections from the other realm are vitally important when each makes his policy decisions or recommendations.

In the absence of a link of understanding, the corporate manager is uniquely handicapped when he tries to carry out his basic and important responsibility—the anticipation of social climate and national economic policy, and the subsequent translation of these into an appropriate influence upon corporate responses. Consider the traditional problem: When the national policy sets a target of a specified mix in growth rate, stability tolerances, employment level, and pricing policy, how does the manager structure the corporate profit objectives, investment plans, and employment projections, in order to serve both *effective corporate survival* and *efficient corporate performance*? There is also the acute problem of the policy direction of *innovation*, which is in this century one of the most important social and economic factors in society. In forming innovation policy, management must consider key factors such as rate and direction of change, potential gains, risks of failure, and destructive effects on existing vested interests. All these have to be evaluated within the framework of both corporate goals and society's objectives.

The present status of corporate accountability jeopardizes both corporate survival and performance. Our society has bred a manager who is beginning to develop a true understanding of how the corporate organism really works, both in its utilization of people and things. It has also bred an array of specialists who are learning more about the workings of our whole political economy and who translate the values of the public consensus into recommendations for action. There is a potential tragedy brewing here, because these two groups of key-decision formers are unable to communicate effectively with each other. It is a situation that imperils the future of our free institutions.

In this situation the missing link is the dimension of accountability. If the answerability of corporate management to society were clearly defined, the definition would necessarily encompass the relationship between corporate policy and public policy.

Some Inadequate Answers

> There is no harm in being sometimes wrong—especially if one is promptly found out.—JOHN MAYNARD KEYNES in *Essays in Biography,* 1933

A perceptive modern manager might be excused for suffering from a recurring nightmare in which he is faced squarely with two dreadful choices. On the one hand, he can be a "profit maximizer," compete "perfectly," and thereby cause proper pricing and allocation, but he may perish in the doing because of a built-in fatal defect in this course of action. The defect is noneconomic in nature; it is rooted in political science, sociology, anthropology, and philosophy. Plainly stated, "pure" maximizing, however effective, is amoral, and in the eyes of the public it is not only nonheroic but finally unacceptable.

On the other hand, the manager can deny the simple garb of a "pure" economic man and assume the mantle of morality and industrial citizenship. Then he causes the allocative and pricing functions in the economy to go seriously awry.

Management has not yet plotted a path out of this dilemma, but others have tried. The more persuasive general structures suggested in recent years will be examined briefly in this section.

The first and foremost is the theory of *pluralism* and *countervailing powers*. It is becoming increasingly clear that the future does not belong to Marxian socialism, as its founder so confidently predicted. It is more likely that it belongs to the highly industrialized, mass-consumption, bureaucratic state, in which the rule-making authority is split up among several groups according to the tenets of pluralism. The result is a system of several—not one and not many, but several—stable power groups, none of which can impose its will unilaterally on the society, but each of which can react against decisions or potential actions that may conceivably harm it.

Riesman, in the sociological surveys preceding the writing of *The Lonely Crowd*, attempted to locate the focal point of power in America, a task that foreign political observers have often attempted unsuccessfully. He considered the collectivity of small businessmen and professional men across the nation who control the Congress; the military men and civilians who control defense and foreign policy; the managers of large corporations, their finance committees, and lawyers, who control private investment and influence the rate of technological change; the big labor leaders who control votes and productivity rates; the Southern politicians who control that quarter of the nation; the organized foreign minorities in the big cities; the editorializers and commentators who shape the public consensus. He concluded:

Power in America seems to me situational and mercurial; it resists attempts to locate it the way a molecule, under the Heisenberg principle, resists attempts simultaneously to locate it and time its velocity.[5]

Out of this pluralistic strife, the concept of "countervailing powers" was born. John Kenneth Galbraith applied the term while at Harvard,[6] although it is a clear descendant of the check-and-balance abstraction originally advocated by John Locke in 1690. In this point of view, the power of the large corporations would be continuously checked by the power of other effective groups. The game would be played, two "teams" at a time, in various arenas: the market, the polls, the courts, the picket lines. Galbraith saw government not only as the umpire in this game, but also as the promoter who should ensure that only well-qualified, relatively equal teams enter the arena.

This concept of countervailing powers has the apparent advantage of relieving each participant of the strain of assuming social responsibility; each group must simply act vigorously and effectively in its own behalf. As a structure that provides accountability, countervailing power is mechanistic, much like Adam Smith's celebrated market system. To those who like to place their trust in impersonal forces (economists among others), it has a natural appeal. For, not only does it reduce the large problem of defining social responsibility and the attendant need to dip far into national and human values, it also has the unassailable virtue that it never requires men to act against their own apparent self-interest.

However, the balance-of-power structure is deficient. Unlike Adam Smith's market system, it suffers because there is confusion about the goal, if any, toward which this oscillating system of beneficial chaos will work. Moreover, the architects of countervailing power underestimated the vigor, the acumen, the assiduity of modern power groups in pursuing their self-interest. The sequence from beneficial strife to impasse to bitter strife to anarchy is a realistic possibility in view of the breakdowns in social and economic process that have characterized the postwar years. In short, this system has the potential to oscillate to the point of self-destruction.

A final flaw has often been suggested. The balance-of-power structure of accountability is uniquely vulnerable to collusion between any two of the effective power groups (say, labor and government, or business and labor).

In a second theory, management has been established as

the trustee for society. The corporation has often been thought of in anthropomorphic terms, that is, as a "man writ large." Like men, it developed its physical self first, and there are those who believe that it will at some point develop a soul, as men have done. Adolf Berle used "conscience of the corporation" to express his belief that corporation managers had become trustees for the entire community rather than simply fiduciaries for the shareholders, as the law still holds. In this broader role of trustee, Berle felt that corporation managers could learn to practice a self-restraint in deference to the balanced needs of the community. This balance would have to include the needs of all segments in the society: employees, shareholders, customers, government, and the community at large. In essence, management would hoist onto its shoulders the burden of *social responsibility*, however the term might be defined.

This concept of accountability sounded good, and it was adopted by some managements. It may be that in some quarters, big stewardship was liked more for its sound than for its intrinsic merits. It allowed the corporation to appear before the public not as a self-seeking profit maximizer, but as a steward of the public interests, accountable for the public good. It was inevitable that some businessmen would accept and use this concept only in its shallow public-relations sense.

The evolution of business thinking toward the position of community trustee has been described in Part I. The gradual decline in recent years of the community trustee attitude in management has resulted from broad problems associated with it. An obvious defect is the almost complete lack of recognition of such a position for management within the statutes of corporate law. The law still holds, severely and simply, that a corporation exists "primarily for the profit of shareholders." Responsible fiduciary management in the interest of the shareholder is still the main plank in new corporation statutes, even in the recent Model Business Corporation Act of the American Bar Association.

Another defect stems from the theory that the trustee is essentially concerned with disbursements from the corporate *usufruct*, a term derived from Roman law and which means "the right of using and enjoying the fruits of an estate or other thing belonging to another, without impairing the substance." As the man holding the keys to the usufruct, as the arbitrator among the claimants, the trustee for the community, and the discharger of social responsibility, the manager finds himself in a morally hazardous position.

First, since he personally is a beneficiary of the corporate usufruct, the manager finds himself as both umpire and player. In equity, in corporate law, in common sense, this is an untenable place for him to be. It is, of course, one of the chief reasons for the original structuring of the corporation, in which the board of directors was established as "not part of the management team," but as an agency of independent review. Wherever the functioning of the directorate has been confused or weakened, this problem of the interested party reasserts itself.

Beyond this lies another hazard. Under the nineteenth-century form of corporate accountability, there were definitive yardsticks to measure the discharge of the responsibility to ownership. But social responsibility is an amorphous concept without clear criteria. How can one define a return to shareholders that is "fair" to the community at large, a wage scale that is socially equitable, a "just" remuneration for management? The social responsibilities have never been defined in a way that makes them a useful guide or criterion for management decisions. Moreover, the public consensus is continually changing its concepts of social obligation.

Some practitioners of management define even tougher burdens:

To the degree that education and other community activities contribute to the success of the company and the society in which it operates, they should and do receive a share of the proceeds.[7]

This statement by Ralph E. Cordiner is one of the broadest conceptions of management's social responsibilities ever pronounced. It implies that management, in dispensing corporate largesse, will undertake to judge the contribution of various activities, not only to the corporation's success but also to society's benefit.

Finally, there is the question of management's charter to operate as a trustee for the community. It has been noted that in law, this charter does not exist. The public consensus however, permits many practices that are not fully sanctioned by the law. For example, the codified picket line practices of organized labor, of questionable legality in some cases, have been permitted for years. Hence the important question concerns the charter from this public consensus. Each time managers speak in public of their duty to arbitrate among the corporation's publics, they unfortunately raise this question of who appointed them. And they invite the inevitable question: If managers are trustees for society, then should not the society participate in their selection and appointment? In retrospect, this idea of the trustee resulted from big thinking, offered significant advantages, but turned out to be replete with pitfalls. As it has been constructed, it imposes intolerable burdens upon the managers. And in its conceptual lack of integrity, it invites intervention.

There is a school of business critics who do not appear to be concerned with the distributions of corporate returns. Instead, they view with alarm the intracorporate environment, which they allege is damaging the capacity of its inhabitants (the employees) to participate as citizens in the national republic. Some names associated with this critical school are Huxley, Orwell, Hutchins, Latham, Buchanan, and C. Wright Mills. These people are in general humanists, and they are for the most part intensely devoted to individualism and personal freedom. They consider bigness in any form to be an enemy that promotes, and is promoted by, a super-abundant growth of organization and technology,[8] which in turn ruthlessly pushes mankind toward a totalitarian control of human mind and spirit, toward the total bleakness of Orwell's *1984*. They propose in general terms that constitutional protection be provided for the citizen *within the corporate organization*. A structure of corporate accountability would thus be instituted in which "due process of law" would apply for all, and a "bill of rights" would be forthcoming. In effect, this is a plan for a homogeneous national political and social structure in which every power subgroup would be structured in the likeness of the national society.

The experienced industrial manager reacts instinctively against this proposed form. Its major flaw lies in its premise that the corporate responsibility for use of economic resources can be divorced from the consideration of corporate responsibility for human beings. The corporation's existence must be justified first in the economic dimension, because it was never intended that the corporation be the agency by which the social aims of the republic would be implemented. Beyond this immediate defense, however, the position of management regarding accountability for corporate effects upon employees is not yet defined. This may be understandable, in view of the imprecise nature of the attacks on this subject, but it is not justifiable, and management must soon establish a position. The human aspect of corporate accountability will be discussed in Chapter 12.

Another substantially sponsored theory demands the resuscitation of ownership. The nineteenth-century structure of corporate accountability possessed several marked advantages: It was well articulated, clear and coherent, solidly founded in the law, and permitted accurate measurements, which indicated the efficiency with which responsibility was discharged. Its problems and its decline stemmed mostly from its negation of social responsibility, its overdrawn reliance upon the mechanistic features of a market system, and importantly from the erosion of its philosophic foundations, as described in Part I. Its attrition was hastened by the wide dispersion of stock ownership.

A refurbished corporate accountability to ownership, exercised only in the economic sphere, is urged strongly by another group. These observers are convinced that corporate organizations should, once and for all, *renounce* social responsibilities. They see the beginning of a massive breakdown of the separation of economic from political powers. They view the modern large business corporation as a superbly efficient, competently staffed organization with large resources available to it. It would be the target for no end of charitable, religious, educational, civic, community, and other projects that need funds, management, resources, know-how, and other corporate assets. If this is social responsibility, then the corporations should accept none of it. This critical group further believes that needy social projects will exploit the well-known guilt feelings, which the businessman has been assiduously educated to feel since 1929–1932. In his yearning to embrace social responsibility, the business manager will move toward an increasingly untenable position, in which he neglects his primary wealth-generating functions while practicing an unwarranted brand of corporate citizenship.

These differing lines of approach end up at the same

point: Corporations should polish up the nineteenth-century model of accountability. But in this matter, there is also a red-ink side of the ledger. If management beats a trail back to the cold tower of "profit maximizing for the shareholders," no matter how rational its position, it may assume a risk it can ill afford—the further damage of the acceptability of its accountability structure.

The last general structure for corporate accountability to be considered here goes under the title "managerialism," conceived by James Burnham in 1940. This was a stepchild disliked and unwanted by its father. His book, *The Managerial Revolution*,[9] presented a case that the manager, because of inevitable forces and unfortunate circumstances, would fall into the controlling position in pluralistic industrial society, whether or not he deserved the position or was qualified for it. Burnham's book generally was an example of hand wringing in which he posited that the managers would turn upon and overthrow the financial interests that had spawned them, and would then become in turn the new exploiters of hapless society. Managers would be self-accountable, but unfortunately only for their own purposes.

This cynical view has been confused by some observers with the totally different concept of a modern profession. Among them are those whose purposes are served by casually merging the distinct ideas of managerialism, social responsibility, and a management profession, and tarring them all with the same brush—professionalism. This term has arisen and has brought with it the traditional meaning; that is, an unrealistic addiction to the professional point of view. It also carries a connotation that those who are addicted are phonies who want the privileges of the true professional without assuming any of the burdens. Observers who use this tar brush do great service to present-day managers, for they point up the perils awaiting the management institution if it ever tries to "promote" its way into professional status by way of the "PR" man and his legerdemain. The dubious art of "how to succeed as a profession without really trying" could lead directly to the demise of much that is valued highly in corporate enterprise.

These, then, are the several principal structures suggested by outside observers for the accountability of managements in a free competitive society. All reflect, to varying degrees, a lack of familiarity on the part of their architects with the actual personal motivations, the roles and sanctions, and the utilization of economic resources within the corporate spheres. Individually or in the aggregate, they do not answer the question that must be answered in the years of this decade. The way is clear for the institution of management to propose its own structure of corporate accountability.

12 Accountability for Human Resources

> And let him know that he who hast undertaken the government of souls, must prepare himself to render an account. And no matter how large the number of brethren that he has under his care may be, let him be absolutely certain that on the day of judgment he is to render an account to the Lord of all these souls, and without doubt likewise of his own.—ST. BENEDICT in *The Rule*, 528 A.D.

Thoughtful men through the years have watched the humanizing forces with admiration tinged with uneasiness. Goethe, writing in 1787, felt that "humanism" would eventually prevail, but was concerned that when it did, "the world will become a huge hospital, with everyone nursing his neighbor." The humanizing forces are devoted to collective man, to the rights of groups of men. From our heritage of political thought, we know that humanizing forces, like all others, must be subject to check and balance. There must be a compensating force, which can be termed the *economizing force*.

The economizing force is a profound concept for the profession of management. Its precise definition will require much work, but for present purposes, it may be considered as the force that causes the efficient *transformation* of the limited material resources of the society into those goods and services desired by society. It implies the optimizing of the output and input relationship, and requires timely informed decisions and unwavering implementation thereof in the economic sphere. Yet the force cannot be construed as mere present-tense economizing; it must be considered in a forward-looking sense, which includes continuous provision for future economizing by means of effective innovation and keen foresight.

Managers, in analyzing the use of the economizing force, run hard onto the core problem of political economy in this century. How is the force most potently applied, by monopolization of economic decision-making authority at central points of power or by dispersal of this authority throughout society? Substantial evidence of the defects in centralized decision making is being compiled in the world. The unfeasibility of centralization is now being confirmed, and terms like "obsolete" are being applied to central planning and control.[1] Management, working with the economists, will professionally confirm that in a mature and complex modern economy, *the economizing force can be applied potently only in an environment where decision making is decentralized within a market structure.*

Therefore it will be found that dedication to the economizing force leads inevitably to higher dedications: first, to freedom within the economic sector, and then to freedom with all its profound meanings in the political sphere. Professional commitment to economic freedom will motivate management to the active support of a well-defined form of competitive enterprise in a broad international market place.

Freedom in economic life is so closely interwoven with human freedom in a more fundamental sense that it is futile to try to distinguish between the two aspects. Freedom in the economic sector is the keystone supporting political freedom; it is a necessary condition even if not by itself sufficient for political freedom.[2] Thus, in the support of economic freedom, the management profession will be carrying its share of the most fundamental Western hopes for the future of man, his freedom, and the release of his mind and spirit to cultivate the purposes for which Providence has placed him on earth. Under these arguments, the economizing force becomes a uniquely appropriate first cause for management at this phase in its history.

The economizing force is one species of the creative or innovative force in man. Where the tasks are large and technically complex, where sophisticated group efforts[3] are required, the modern professions become in Western societies the unique shelter of these forces. To incubate these fragile drives, to shield them from diversions, the professions tend to be nonsocial in outlook. To make the point, they often stand for excellence at the cost of equality and for individuality over conformity. This professional outlook on the purposes of work must be constructively blended with the opposing forces to form the public consensus, to select the public goals.

Herein lies a problem in understanding for the emergent profession of management. The problem is of some depth, and it demands that all professional managers find their own paths to understanding.

The Economizing Philosophy

Philosophy is nothing but discretion.—JOHN SELDEN, 1689

There are philosophical concepts that can help us understand how to combine the economizing and humanizing forces in the political economy, and which can lead to an understanding of how corporate managements can be both effective and accountable. The first concept, the most difficult in its abstraction, is drawn from the fields of physics, thermodynamics, and statistical mechanics, and is referred to as *entropy*. In recent years, partially as a result of Norbert Wiener's construction of the science of cybernetics, entropy has been found to have applications in organizational science.[4] In physics, the energy within a closed system is available from heat differentials; the smaller these differentials, the smaller the available energy. It is fundamental that in any closed system, the differentials tend to decrease, and therefore any such system gradually runs down, reaches a final state of heat equilibrium in which there is no energy, and deteriorates into formless chaos. Scientists, in a mood of cosmic pessimism, view the universe as a closed system, gradually degenerating.

Entropy, as it is applied here, is this general tendency of a system to run down. In any physical, closed thermal system, entropy always increases, and as it increases, it attacks the system. The systems of prime interest to people, however, are not closed or isolated, but rather are connected (or "coupled," as the scientists say) with other systems in their environment. An active volcano is a system that has been well coupled with a heat differential or energy source and thereby becomes what Wiener calls an "island of locally decreasing entropy" in a general universe where entropy is increasing. For whatever purpose Providence designed the volcano (perhaps to relieve dangerous stresses within the crust of the earth), it is an effective instrument. Thus it is purposeful, energetic, vital, even orderly; all these are antientropic physical conditions existing in a universe where in the majority of situations the opposite adjectives apply.

How is the concept of entropy used in organizational science? Heat and energy were related to physics, but in recent years scientists have been able to associate *energy* with *information*. In a political or economic organism, say, a federal type of government, there may be some few cells that are highly coupled in the reception and transmission of real information, which utilize this information well in determining their own behavior and become in effect local zones of energy and purpose. These few are the entropy-reducing subunits in the whole organism, and they are the agents not only of growth but also of survival. They effect their own survival and also that of the whole organism *if there are enough of them.* These few successful antientropic subunits, the lifegivers, develop a method of *learning* from their environment. This enables them to stand up to the entropic stream of corruption and decay, to rebuild their successful pattern faster than the stream can tear it down.

Every corporate manager can grasp the concept of entropy because he has seen its destructive effects in his experience. He finds that in the representative large multidivision corporation only a very few departments are the life givers. He knows that within the usual department, only a few individuals inject vitality and purpose. In the advanced technology industries, he has seen the demon of entropy take over large laboratories that originally fulfilled great purposes. He suspects that, among the very many organizations that exist in the American socioeconomic structure, a fraction of a per cent of individuals are the entropy reducers.

Another concept relevant to the present environment of corporate management has been contributed by the profound insights of Paul Tillich, professor of theology at Harvard. Tillich's construction of the concept of the *demonic*[5] is a support to those who must act and be responsible for results. In the demonic concept, every creative human act produces an inseparable mixture of good and evil. The activist, the seeker after good results, must assume the risks of interwoven evil if he would accomplish. An illustration in industry is the process of technological innovation: The power loom led to the destruction of the hand weaver's craft, of his way of life. Each new innovation will eliminate the value of existing real capital, which technically might be usable for many more years. Each time a manager is creative, he is destructive.

Tillich notes that great creative force was released when economics became autonomous; that is, when it was separated from political and religious power and influences. This creativity was hugely supplemented when the outputs of technical science and the mechanism of the free market were added to it, and competitive capitalism became "the most successful form of production of goods which has ever existed." But Tillich also points out that "this creative force is combined with a destructive one of horrible strength . . . the depth of the demonic is just this, that the meaningful and meaningless elements in it are inseparably combined."

This enmeshed evil spawned the child labor pits and the sweat shops; it has been attenuated, but it still lurks always in the process of economizing. The evil emerges whenever the humanizing forces are overridden.

The economizing force may be viewed as one of the primary entropy-reducing factors in a political economy. Like all antientropic forces, it is applied by a small minority of all the groups in society, and although it is very powerful, it is also easily damaged. Where shall the modern Western societies seek the fountainhead of the economizing force? The West may choose to place the force under political overseers, as in the postwar British experiments, where it will be watched so well that it tends to smother if not expire. In this case, a flood of entropy is loosed within the economy, and it is feasible that the few economically creative units may be washed under.

Conversely, the West may choose to leave the economizing force unguided and subject to the net push and pull of the grinding confrontation of countervailing powers. Or, in their third choice, Western societies may choose a mean course in which they turn over the force to a profession of men who will apply it in a pragmatic but also a guided manner. This guidance will stem from the knowledgeability of a professional institution, which is effectively accountable to the public. The pragmatism will emerge from the profession's dedication to the free market, and will provide the flexibility that will permit the force to be used in accord with changing public goals.

In this case, both the new management profession and the modern corporation will become microspheres in society which are the shelters for antientropic actions, a home for the economizing force. They will become this, not because they are *like* the macrosphere of society, but because they are *unlike* it. And the professional man will have also cultivated his unlikeness to the prototype under the social ethic: He will be a disciple of individualism and rationalism. In his conduct he will be traditional and conservative, speaking only on matters where he is informed and dealing with other human beings according to a strict code that abhors dogma and avoids appeal to the emotions. Yet, in the practice of his special discipline, professional man will be a radical who continuously innovates and breaks with tradition.

The concept of the demonic also relates directly to the economizing force. Good managers have long known that they must be prepared to respond to, and live with, unanticipated situations developing from their actions in prosecution of economizing goals. Decisions that breed intended positive results have often simultaneously bred unexpected adverse conditions, as the concept of the demonic predicts. A wide-awake awareness of this constant potentiality, a philosophical acceptance of it, a willingness to react vigorously to counter the adversity when it happens, all these will be indispensable attributes of the manager each time he must venture away from his science into the area of his professional art.

Return now to the question of merging the professional outlook, with its economizing bias, with the opposing socially biased forces in the public consensus. This can be a constructive synthesis, or conversely, it can be destructively misguided and can result in the crippling of the economizing force. Such a destructive synthesis would be a victory for those who would destroy Western culture. *Moderation*, of a very knowledgeable nature, is the prescription.

Man has long realized that he should not be an extremist, that in all his life he must select his way between opposing principles. In the Hindu writings of the second century before Christ, one can find this advice: "You must be free from the pairs of opposites."[6] During the recent age of black-and-white ideology, the virtuous mean was neglected. In 1932, Abbott Lawrence Lowell, president of Harvard wrote a short but impressive volume in which he reminded his fellow men that abstract principles must not be evaluated in terms of whether they are true or false.[7] The real question is *how far* are they true. *To what extent* does the inherent truth in a given principle justify its extension and application in each changing circumstance? Aristotle said that moral good is served by the mean, that both defect and excess are vices, the former falling short of what is right, the latter exceeding what is right. President Lowell added: "A great part of the art of life and of civilization lies in ascertaining the true limits of conjugate principles."

This philosophy of the mean has a clear application to the problem of corporate responsibility. The question is no longer which structures are right. Social responsibility is right, and profit maximizing is right. The real effort to be made is in determining the true limits of the several sets of

polar principles interwoven in the subject of corporate
accountability. Professional managers know that Western
societies must seek a virtuous mean as the net prevailing
balance in their political economies. From the managers'
point of view, extreme socializing bias is defect, and extreme
economizing bias is excess. Managers will sponsor the economizing force, and they will be accountable for its preservation. The way in which they form their practice and become
accountable for the use of human beings in enterprise will
help determine the synthesis with the humanizing drives.

Participation and Progress

> The exploration and development of means whereby the
> American economic system can best satisfy its two impera-
> tives—democracy and full effectiveness under the new con-
> ditions—is an important and challenging goal for Americans
> in the 1960's.—CLARK KERR in *The Report of the President's
> Commission on National Goals,* 1960

Among the receipts that the employee expects today are
an increasingly progressive distribution of corporate income,
personal treatment within the corporation which is "right"
by changing standards, protection, status, various forms of
security, a pleasant work environment, diversion, and education. As contemporary companies approach this model in
varying degrees, an observer may find the following manifestations:

The employee spends his leisure hours at a country club built
and maintained by his company. He furthers his education in
part-time curricula conducted or sponsored by the company; his
children compete for company scholarships at universities. His
charitable contributions are influenced or established by company policies. His personal estate-planning function is inextricably mingled with his company's offices, in the matters of life

and health insurance, pension, deferred compensation, even borrowing of funds for personal use. In a growing number of ways, his socio-economic future is a function, not of the relationship between his competency and the community economy, but of this committed personal-corporate relationship.

The employee becomes a citizen of the corporation, in this limiting case of the twentieth-century model of accountability. As citizenship becomes his lot, the corporation demands his total loyalty. It crosses the hazy line that separates an economic organization from a political government. But it is all for an originally good purpose, for the corporation now assumes responsibilities in several forms for the human beings in its whole environment. This polar model of corporate accountability for the use of human souls is not simple, it is exercised in varying degrees within three dimensions: political, social, and economic.

The economizing force requires much hard work, which can come only from human beings. The point is emphasized in every industrializing nation in which the force is going through its difficult adolescence. In these nations there is a common problem[8]: How can people be made to work harder? In India, Egypt, and in the communist regimes, there are native versions of the Anglo-Saxon hard work ethic which sparked the leap to industrialization by the Western nations.

There will always be heavy pressure upon industrial managers to succumb to production needs and override human needs. When managers do succumb, they set up an *excess* of economizing. A profession, being a vehicle of dynamic moderation, will seek the limiting mean between excess and defect. This cannot be done negatively by any theory of mere *accommodation* to the humanizing forces. It can be done positively by the continuous acquisition of professional knowledge about the human being and the small group within the environment of the industrial corporation. The time is ripe for a real joint effort by practitioners of industrial administration and social scientists in the behavioral disciplines. The result of this effort can be a workable understanding of the utilization of human resources in industry.

Social scientists tend to regard this as a problem that requires the enlightenment of management. They find that some contemporary managements are burdened with fallacious theories of human behavior.[9] For example, some of these theories are that pecuniary gain is the only real incentive that motivates employees; that men are naturally lazy; that class struggle is natural to men; and that power is the only effective means of control in an organization. One camp in the trade union leadership follows the same outworn theories; this group represents the "company is always trying to rob us" faction.[10] Managers who persist in applying these theories are not professional. Neither were the physicians of the past century who persisted in applying "bleeding and purging" for a variety of ills, even after some of their colleagues had demonstrated the lack of validity of the theories underlying this practice.

Analysts have demonstrated that the effectiveness of a management depends on the concept of human relationships in which that management believes. Most managements devote considerable attention to the latest findings of social scientists, and each year United States industry commits much time and money to "human relations" seminars and studies. But the new concepts are not taking hold. A prominent research team from the University of California's Institute of Industrial Relations, which has completed a recent international survey of the real attitudes of executives, makes this comment:

Ideas dealing with management practice have been persuasive, while the basic conviction about the nature of people remains unchanged. It is a little like building the techniques and practices of a Jeffersonian democracy on a basic belief in the divine right of kings.[11]

Behavioral scientists are asking managers to get the right picture of the human being in industry. The right picture is the one that emerges from scientific investigation and experiment with real conditions and from the cooperative efforts of professional managers and scientists.

The right picture of human behavior within the corporation has changed profoundly since the beginning of economic society. Broadly speaking, the range of Western outlook on industrial relations has evolved from the *dictatorial* concept to the *paternalistic* to the *democratic* to the present emphasis upon the *participative*. Lawrence Appley has graphically expanded this progression in human relationships:

Savagery—the other fellow is my enemy and to be destroyed.

Slavery—the other fellow is to be conquered and put at my service.

Servitude—the other fellow is to serve me for consideration and ask no more.

Welfare—the other fellow should be helped up when down, without too much concern for what got him down.

Paternalism—the other fellow should be cared for, and I will decide to what extent.

Participation—the other fellow has something to contribute to my efforts and can help me.

Trusteeship—that for which I am responsible is not mine. I am developing and administering it for the benefit of others.

Statesmanship—the other fellow is capable of being far more than he is, and it is my responsibility to help him develop to his fullest potential.[12]

Is the criticism from social scientists, which they have justified on the basis of observations of corporate conditions, an indictment of the morality of management? Apparently it is not. It is rather an indictment of the competence and perception of management within its own field. It is *knowledge* and *practice* that are impugned, two elements of a profession. What is being said is that management first does not know and then does not practice the right way to human productivity in industrial enterprise. This is not a judgment in the moral sphere; it is simply a criticism of the professional capacity of management.

As managers gain full understanding of the true nature of participative industrial relations, they will become committed to the continual development of corporate human resources to higher levels of effectiveness. They will also progressively expand their use of these developed human resources in decision making. This will be a transition of basic importance because, for the first time since the days of laissez faire, the prevailing human relations concept will serve both the economizing process and the mores of society. Effective and highly developed employees in increasing numbers further the ends of economic productivity, while at the same time, they are a favorable response to the social demands of the public consensus.

But this transition to a higher plane of utilization of human resources can take place only if management fully develops its *professional understanding* of human behavior in industry. Several emerging scientific disciplines will foster this knowledge: organization theory, industrial psychology, communications theory, among others, and also several key industrial fields of study stemming from the traditional disciplines of political science, cultural anthropology, sociology, and philosophy. Managers will have a responsibility of knowledge in these areas, equivalent to their old traditional responsibilities (that is, finance and control) and their new traditional responsibilities (that is, data processing).

Avoidance of Modern Feudalism

> The virtue of leaving considerable economic power in private hands is not too dissimilar from the virtue of leaving considerable political power in the several states of a federation . . . both reject centralism because of the bureaucratic overload at best, the political and moral overload at worst, which total accountability to central authority portends.—KINGMAN BREWSTER, JR. in *The Corporation in Modern Society,* 1959

Some insurance companies have recently included key paragraphs in their circulars to managers who are prospects, exhorting these managers not to allow a large portion of their personal insurance portfolios to reside in company insurance programs. The circulars hint that an executive whose insurance is heavily apportioned to company-vested plans thereby loses certain freedoms of action and even may have to compromise his principles upon occasion. In short, they imply that he loses the economic freedom to quit. These circulars spotlight a small part of a big problem, which not ten top managers out of one hundred are concerned about now. Within a few years the subject may be of prime concern to the majority of managers.

This growing problem arises from management's efforts to take care of employees, to develop their talents, to provide security in employment, security in retirement, and security against misfortune. In pursuit of this type of social responsibility, management may yield to many temptations and set up an *excess* of beneficial processes.

The potential evil may be the reconstruction of a feudalism that waits at the end of the line. "Every company's long-term debt to its employees" inevitably breeds a long-term obligation in the reverse direction. The base pattern of ancient feudalism was allegiance, fealty, total loyalty. This pattern covered all dimensions of human living: political, economic, social, and religious. But *the feudal pattern did not foster the human attitudes and talents that were later found necessary for industrial enterprise under capitalism.* In feudalism, as in communism, the individual has no freedom of dissociation or change in his economic life, and his whole life is thereby restricted.

Labor has often urged that management assume the more general responsibilities for job continuity. As an example, if a corporation has subcontracted for years to firms in City X, it should assume responsibility for employment conditions in those firms and that city.[13] Implicitly, it would breach its obligations if it caused discontinuity of employment in that city, say, by changing subcontractors.

When I discussed this peril for the corporation with an eminent academic administrator who is a director of major companies, his comments were:

Corporate managements still try to inculcate total loyalty in their people, like some of the old proprietors used to attempt. However, now the methods are more sophisticated and more persuasive. *But this effort is the biggest mistake modern management can make.* I never like to try anything which, if I succeed in it, will kill me. Yet that's exactly what these managements are doing.

Outside observers now like to characterize the business corporation as a "quasi-political institution." If our corporations become private governments, they will find that our American kind of people make tough citizens. They demand more of their government than any corporation can give and still remain an effective wealth-generating organization. Managers don't understand, and scholars don't point out to them, that there is one basic reason why corporations can never be governments. And the reason is that the original association of a person with an industrial corporation is *voluntary;* it's not by birth, indenture, slavery, or any other involuntary means. It's just not like citizenship.

I realize the investment that companies have tied up in their people, particularly certain kinds of people. But total loyalty and citizenship are still very dangerous ideas inside a corporation. The employee still must be able to realize many of his satisfactions outside the corporation. And he needs to be able to leave when he has to.

It is precisely this problem of overcommitted loyalty, in both directions, that the humanists fear may lead to the eventual dissolution of human spirit. It is the problem that sparked their vigorous attack, already described here, and which maintains that attack. William H. Whyte, Jr., a spokesman for the humanist school, puts it this way:

No one wants to see the old authoritarian return, but at least it could be said of him that what he wanted primarily from you was your sweat. The new man wants your soul.[14]

Clark Kerr, chancellor of the University of California, counsels in this manner:

The danger is not that loyalties are divided today but that they may be undivided tomorrow . . . I would urge each individual to avoid total involvement in any organization . . . to struggle against the effort to absorb.[15]

Thus the headlong push of the 1950s into social responsibility and managerial "arbitration" among the interests of the publics has developed unforeseen results. The specific hazards to the corporate institution may be latent to most, but they become visible in outline to a perceptive few. Continuing drive by management, abetted by organized labor, toward a feudal device—the total-security social-economic-political corporation—may well bring an unwanted response in the form of total external regulation by statute and agency.

Present straws in the wind portend the nature of these regulatory actions:

Proposals are made regularly to introduce, by federal mandate, certain provisions of American civil law into the corporate sphere. Chief among these provisions are a "bill of rights" for all corporate citizens (referred to as "corporate constitutionalism") and more importantly, suffrage and "due process of law."

Other critics cite the features of a workable federal union, which require that there be a power outside the state which ensures fair treatment of the citizens inside it. Also, federalism requires that there be no *substantial barriers* to the free movement of people among several states. Following this line of thought, they suggest the enactment of laws which prohibit discriminatory features in deferred compensation, stock option, and retirement plans which tend to hold key employees within one company.

One primary hazard to the corporation looms above the others. Probably most managers concur in the prevailing belief of Western thought that human virtue is an individual and personal thing. An institution, (say, a profession) can enhance inherent virtue in young men entering it by means of institutional standards. But virtue and integrity are not the products of any institution, and in Western mores a *main role* of governance is to provide the environment in which virtue can be developed and practiced by each citizen.

An institution may unfortunately nurture loyalties to it that constrain personal virtue or which maim the capacity of its members to live as virtuous citizens of their political state. For many reasons, corporations, labor unions, and other contemporary institutions can fall prey to this over-developed loyalty. But it is a grievous mistake, and it will ultimately prove to be unforgivable in the eyes of American public opinion. Hence the inhibition of individual virtue in any way within the corporation becomes a cardinal sin, and the management profession must so recognize it in defining corporate accountability for human resources.

The advocates of the corporate bill of rights are in reality asking for a completely homogeneous political structure in which each organization would be a political microcosm closely resembling the national macrocosm. Thus all organizational decisions in the land would in some way involve suffrage and the individual vote. Nowhere in the words of the founding fathers of the United States, in the books of philosophy, or in law or common sense can these advocates find support for this great political sameness they desire in American organizations. But beyond this, sameness fosters organizational entropy, and entropy implies the rate of approach of organizational death.

As indicated earlier, a society must possess a sufficient number of entropy-reducing subunits within it, or it cannot survive and grow. Any manager of industrial experience, whether or not he has ever heard of entropy, knows that constitutionalism and suffrage within the industrial corporation will cause its death.

How can the offense of the constitutionalists be blunted? It can be negated by a philosophic truth which they themselves have used. Corporate purposes and industrial productivity are not the end objectives of life; they are merely important means to a greater end. Corporations are not governments; they do not have citizens; and it was never intended that "due process" be applied within them.

The demanding complexities of the corporation's economic mission preclude due process and suffrage. An analogy will emphasize the point:

The *block structure* of society, in which there is no social mobility of persons between blocks, is totally out of keeping with the American character. Yet it is exemplified in the modern hospital, where nurse, doctor, and orderly are each members of a social block with no prospect of migration between blocks. To the present writer's knowledge, there has never been any clamor from the humanists regarding this breach of American ideals; they have not advocated political homogeneity which includes this type of American organization. They also understand that constitutionalism and suffrage, if introduced into the hospital, would destroy the hospital's reason for existence. During surgery, there may be consultations, to be sure, but there is no voting.[16]

The projection of management accountability for human resources can now be briefly recapitulated. People within industry would be "used" essentially to maintain and sharpen the economizing force. Irresponsible critics will say that this use is Machiavellian and manipulative. On the contrary it would be socially desirable, for several reasons. First, the economizing force as maintained in Western culture is a necessary keystone to support both freedom and order, and the employment of human brain and brawn in support of such a force would be required and commendable. Second, management can preserve the functioning of the free market so that the economizing force would provide those goods and services that the public wants. Third, management would be responsible for using people in industry in the way that people work most effectively. Fourth, management would develop the capacities of corporate employees and would expand its utilization of their skills and abilities. The last two aims can be achieved by means of professional management competency in the fields of human behavior and the organizational sciences.

In this accountability, constitutionalism should be recognized to the extent that the "rights" of employees would be formalized and honored. These rights should include the right to share appropriately in the corporate yields, the right to self-fulfillment and personal growth. However, in pursuing social aims, the profession should establish a limit which it will not exceed. Management would help its employees develop, and would observe their rights, but only in the furtherance of their company's economic purposes and not out of a sense of indissoluble bond or feudal fealty connecting the employees to the company. Management would avoid encroaching upon the whole lives of the employees; it would not demand corporate citizenship or total loyalty. It would ever be conscious that corporate purposes are but a means to an end. It would fight by all ethical means the introduction of due process and suffrage into the corporation.

13 Practice of Accountability

Our challenge, then, is to roll up our sleeves and get to work. We will not make the world perfect, but we can work hard at making it better, at making our system serve its people better than any other. Our goal is to keep moving the standards ahead, solid step by solid step, year in and year out, each business by itself, each man quietly, sincerely, effectively.—Louis W. Cabot, President, Cabot Corporation, writing in *The Stanford Business Bulletin,* 1962

At present, large problem areas in Western economic society are painfully evident. It is to these topical areas that the emergent management profession must address itself when it begins the task of many years in building a detailed professional accountability. The solution to these problems can be advanced by the application of detailed understanding of the economizing process, the kind of understanding developed only by the manager experienced in the corporate sphere.

The broad problem areas in which corporate management becomes accountable for contributing its share to the resolution include the following seven situations:

1. Maintenance of entrepreneurial vitality; preservation and improvement of the international free market within the Western world; refinement of both the knowledge *and*

149

the know-how of modern corporate competition; building of entropy-reducing economic units within the society.

2. Intelligent and effective use of human resources in the corporate sector; appropriate application of the behavioral sciences in industrial administration; integration of diverse human efforts into complex industrial projects; synthesis of the economizing force with social objectives, and bilateral definition of obligations between corporations and employees.

3. Continuous improvement of *productivity* in the provision of goods and services, with the minimum use of resources; refinement of the measurement of productivity; defining the relationship of human skills and capital facilities in augmenting productivity; analysis of corporate profits as an indicator of the effectiveness of production; establishment of wage standards and incentives in relation of productivity.

4. Synthesis of corporate decisions with national and international macroeconomics; effective allocation of resources; corporate response to fiscal and monetary policies, effects of government spending, and reconciliation of government revenue requirements with a nondistorting tax structure; the "imperative of growth" and what it means at the corporate level; debt discipline and budgeting of macrocosmic expenditures; role of profit within the corporation and role of aggregate corporate profits in growth and stability of the economy; effects of corporate dividend and depreciation policies upon the macroeconomic picture.

5. Refinement of the clear legitimacy of management authority in the corporation and maintenance thereof by means of an appropriate succession mechanism; attunement of managerial authority with the sociopolitical environment; interprofession relationships with economists, lawyers, academicians, politicians, and intellectuals; refinement of the roles of the directorate and holders of voting stock.

6. Exploitation and control of technological innovation in its impact upon corporate enterprise; role of research and development in the creation of enterprise; integration of defense R & D with the national economy; obsolescence of mass production, and the concept of the unsaturable *idea* market versus the saturable *thing* market.

7. Interrelationship between the *educational process* and the economizing process; effectiveness of education and training, both within and outside the corporation, in the enlargement of human capacity to contribute to the economizing process; optimum function of the graduate professional management school; needs and prospects for successful *retraining* of the employee displaced because of technological immobility or geographic immobility; strengthening of the attack upon economic illiteracy, within and outside the corporations.

These seven major problem areas constitute the field of practice for the new profession. But more importantly for the purposes of this writing, they define the scope of the profession's responsibility. Every manager must become specially competent in at least one of the problem areas so that the profession may be expertly represented in all. In each area the profession will have to answer these crucial questions:

What is the management professions's share of the burden in the resolution of this problem?

How will the profession discharge its share of the responsibility?

With what other authorities must the management profession cooperate in resolving the problem, and how?

The mechanisms and agencies that will be used in building

this accountability are not yet fully clear, but they will surely evolve behind the principles and the motivation. A redefined accountability requires first a professional discipline of management, demonstrating the key elements: knowledge, a successful practice, a governing ethic, and an effectual dedication. All these together constitute accountability. A manager who is deficient in any one cannot be effectively accountable.

This professional discipline can be built over a standing foundation, just as modern nuclear physics has retained elements from Newtonian physics. Today's managers will retain the sound concepts they have inherited—the pragmatic regard for the wisdom of the free market, the sanctity of service and the zeal for success in the calling, the hard work ethic, the ingenuity in overcoming obstacles, the will to break with tradition and to experiment. Above this foundation, there is much building to be done.

The profession of management at last can supply the modern link between public and corporate policies. The bridge will be built by a practicing management profession. As this profession grows with the caliber of practitioners, a new asset must come into being: This may be termed *management capital*, an available and urgently needed know-how that is surplus to the immediate needs on the firing line within the corporations, know-how that can be plowed back into the whole economy to nurture future growth. The profession will *assume its share of responsibility* for the health of the economy, much as the medical vocation learned in 1910 that there was also a preventive function of crucial importance in medicine.

The mind of the professional manager will be indoctrinated to focus primarily on the specific problems he faces in his practice, but he must also be alert to transcend them, to think next to the effect on his community, his industry, the national economy, and the general potency of the economizing force. Professional industrial managers will begin to serve regularly in two distinct capacities. First, the majority of them will at any one time be hard at work within the corporations. Second, a substantial group of them will be practicing management outside the corporations, at locations where management capital needs to be invested. These locations will be in federal and state government agencies, in other public agencies and administrative authorities, and in the academic environment where managers receive professional education. The corporations will cooperate, so that managers whose services are desired in these locations will be able to move and return to the corporate sector with facility.

An obvious precaution must be restated. Management will hold that men who are running a corporation cannot in general make any allowance in their decision making for economic goals outside the corporation, whenever they perceive these goals as noneconomic for their firms. That is, the dictates of the firm's performance and survival must be accommodated first by those managers who are practicing within that firm. If a 5 per cent national growth rate is specified as a national goal, the managers of a given corporation cannot support this goal by any measures that would adversely affect the survival or performance potential of that firm.

How will the bridge of understanding be built? The managers who are serving in the society outside the companies, who have previously served well within a company or companies, who understand interfirm phenomena, who will later return to the corporations—these men will bridge the gap. They will be fully accomplished as professional overseers of wealth-generating operations inside the corporations *before* they assume these posts, and they will be expected to return to the corporations. They will know how to meet a payroll, but they will also know much more. They will inject a comprehensive knowledge of microeconomics into macroeconomic planning. They can be professionally disinterested to the extent that their counsel is sought with regard to aggregate profits and the over-all health of the economy—in short, the potency of the economizing force.

These men will communicate at a professional level with their associates who practice in the private sector of the economy. National policy will come to influence private policy, and corporate planning will be knowledgeably reflected in national planning. The schizophrenic attitude of managers toward planning will be relieved, as will the strains resulting therefrom. Managers practicing in the public sector will work positively with the economists and other specialists in government, and knowledgeable national planning and decision making will induce societal economic policy within the corporations in the aggregate. At the same time, there will be minimal need for compromise of the economic objectives of individual companies.

Thus *management capital* will set up a vast network of communications and motivations among knowledgeable professionals. The network will be maintained informally yet effectively, and will cut across the barriers that separate public and private policy. Although the immediate and near-term aims of these professionals will often be divergent, to an extent depending on their current responsibilities, the common devotion to the economizing process will provide a basis for merging these aims. And, as long as the practitioners are truly qualified professionals, they will be able to make these necessary reconciliations.

These are the ways in which a comprehensive accountability structure will be built for professional management so that it covers all major responsibility areas. This new accountability will be a product of moderation, but it will be tough-minded and practical. It will seek to blend the virtues of humanizing with the imperatives of economizing, but it will not be an all-things-to-all-claimants kind of responsibility. It will recognize that a management decision for one purpose will often be a decision against some other purpose.

The time is late for management to assert itself in shaping its own destiny and that of the corporate institution. In some lands of the Western culture, managers appear to have resigned themselves to reacting to the next restriction imposed and to have little energy for the assertion of management concepts.

Yet, in the past, Western cultures have produced the kind of leaders they needed. In America, the Colonial era abounded with men of political insights and abilities. Later, when the continent's resources had to be developed, the nation produced its dynamic empire builders. In the years since the scientific revolution ushered in the age of analysis, the West has been blessed with ample scientific genius. Now, in the so-called Age of Synthesis, when we try to put back together that which the analysts have dissected, on what group of men will the mantle fall?

Management, in successfully building a broad practicing profession and a viable self-accountability, will become the last potent defender of freedom in the economic sphere. And, if freedom in its economic dimension falls prey to totalitarian control, all other aspects of human liberation and self-development in the political, religious, and social dimensions will soon follow. Thus management finds itself manning a key bastion of human freedom. Seldom does any institution of men have the opportunity to assume the proportions, and the obligations, of the heroic. History verifies that the heroic, once assumed, has one commanding feature —it nearly always works.

Notes

2. ORIGINS

1. See Max Weber, *Protestant Ethic and the Spirit of Capitalism*, and the Foreword by R. H. Tawney (New York: Chas. Scribner's Sons, 1948).
2. Bertrand Russell, *Portraits from Memory* (London: George Allen & Unwin Ltd., 1956), p. 3.
3. These are references to the corporate form in the laws of Solon, sixth century B.C. In Plutarch's writing, there is reference to a Numa Pompilius (715–672 B.C.) who is stated to have conceived the idea of incorporation.
4. See I. Maurice Wormster, *Frankenstein, Incorporated* (New York: McGraw-Hill Book Company, 1931), Wormser quotes from Sohm, *Institutes of Roman Law* (Oxford: Clarendon Press, London, New York, etc. H. Frowde, 1907), to establish that the Roman legal approach to the corporation was a "veritable masterpiece of juristic ingenuity." Also, Sir Henry Maine, in his classic *Ancient Law: Its Connection with the Early History of Society and Its Relation to Modern Ideas*, 16th ed. (New York: Oxford University Press, 1931), comments upon the contributions of the Roman law to the development of the corporation.
5. William Z. Ripley, in his *Main Street and Wall Street* (Boston: Little Brown & Company, 1932), p. 61, quotes Sir James Coke, a legal writer of the early seventeenth century, who had set forth the opinion of a peer of the realm about corporations—that they were "invisible, immortal, having no conscience or soul—and therefore no subpoena lieth against them; they cannot speak nor appear in person, but by attorney."
6. Thomas Hobbes, *Leviathan*, Part II, "Of Commonwealth," in *Man and the State: The Political Philosophers*. Edited by Saxe Commins and R. N. Linscott. (New York: Random House, Inc., 1947). Chapter XXIX.

7. The English common law in its prudery long refused to recognize the existence of corporations among the citizenry, and in fact considered it a crime for men "to presume to act as a corporation." However, for centuries the English circumvented the intent of the common law by resorting to forming "trusts" under private law and the courts of equity.

8. In 1718, the regent of France, in financial distress, grasped at the speculative scheme of a Scotsman, John Law, who was allowed to organize a wild venture known as the Mississippi Company. The purpose was to exploit the "mountains of gold" on the new American continent. The boom was extreme, and speculators fought for the privilege of buying stock. When the jerry-built structure finally and suddenly collapsed in 1720, there remained a few private fortunes, in the hands of those who had sold out in time, and thousands of ruined speculators.

    In 1720, the English Parliament granted monopoly privileges to the South Sea Company in return for the company's taking over £30 million of the national debt. The public's conception of the vast wealth in gold and silver in Spanish America provided a base for easy exploitation by stock manipulators. Within three months, the stock had been bid from £100 per share to its peak of £1060. Unscrupulous speculators used the resulting bull market to promote stock in fictitious or worthless ventures. The collapse of the Mississippi Company bubble in France shook the English market, and suddenly Britain had its own bubble disaster. In the wake of the financial ruin, the entire government was discredited, and there followed a period of successive scandals.

9. These phrases are from an advertisement in *Collier's Weekly*, March 7, 1908, lauding the advantages of incorporation in the territory of Arizona.

3. NINETEENTH-CENTURY MODEL

1. The entire modern version of the American adaptation is systematically treated by the National Association of Manufacturers in *The American Individual Enterprise System* (2 vols.) (New York: McGraw-Hill Book Company, 1946). Also, academic comment upon this topic is set forth in Sutton, Harris, *et al.*, *The American Business Creed* (Cambridge: Harvard University Press, 1956).

2. Lorin F. Deland, *Imagination in Business* (New York: Harper & Brothers, 1909).

3. National Association of Manufacturers, *op. cit.*, Vol. II, Chapter XII, pp. 595 ff.

4. EROSION OF ACCOUNTABILITY

1. See Joseph A. Schumpeter, *Capitalism, Socialism and Democracy* (New York: Harper & Brothers, 1942), pp. 75 ff.
2. William H. Whyte, Jr., *The Organization Man* (New York: Doubleday & Company, Inc., 1957) and David Riesman, Nathan Glazer, *et al.*, *The Lonely Crowd*, 1950.
3. The noted legal philosopher Bertrand de Jouvenel in his 1957 book, *Sovereignty: An Inquiry into the Political Good*, advances the thesis that a legislative tyranny has formed over the democratic peoples of the world.
4. These data are from *The 17 Million, 1962 Census of Shareowners in America*, published by the New York Stock Exchange, 1963.
5. Robert A. Gordon, *Business Leadership in the Large Corporation* (Washington, D. C.: The Brookings Institution, 1945). In Chapter II, extensive use is made of data from Temporary National Economic Committee, Monograph No. 29, "The Distribution of Ownership in the 200 Largest Non-Financial Corporations."
6. *Ibid.*, p. 45. This conclusion is roughly in accord with the 1932 study by Berle and Means, *The Modern Corporation and Private Property* (New York: The Macmillan Company, 1934), p. 115, in which they state that 34 per cent of the 200 large companies they observed were controlled through ownership.
7. See *The Outlook*, published by Standard and Poor's Corporation, Vol. 32, No. 40 (Oct. 3, 1960), pp. 602 ff.

5. TWENTIETH-CENTURY MODEL

1. Before this act, top industrial wages in the United States had generally not exceeded $2.50 for a 9-hour day. A very good account of Ford's board meeting on January 1, 1914, is contained in R. L. Bruckberger, *Image of America* (New York: The Viking Press, 1959), p. 195.
2. *Dodge* v. *Ford Motor Co.* 204 Michigan 459, 170 N.W. 668 (1919), p. 684.
3. See Sutton, Harris, *et al.*, *The American Business Creed* (Cambridge: Harvard University Press, 1956), for a comprehensive treatment of these two versions.
4. The twentieth-century model of corporate accountability is probably that which would prevail in Richard Eells' "metrocorporation." See Eells, *The Meaning of Modern Business* (New York: Columbia University Press, 1960), Chapter III, "The Metrocorporation." In this pioneering and scholarly environmental analysis of the corporation, he sets up the metrocorporation as

a heuristic model of a business unit that has gone "all the way" in accommodating the social and political demands of the present. This corporation becomes in effect an identical microcosm of the state. In defining an organization of this nature, the author outlines a compatible type of managerial accountability. It might be posited that the kind of accountability determines the corporation, and that the general practice of twentieth-century accountability as depicted in Chapter 4 would lead to the emergence of an organization very much like Eells' metrocorporation.

5. Thomas Hobbes, in *Leviathan,* and Jean-Jacques Rousseau, in *The Social Contract* (New York: Hafner Library of Classics No. 1, 1954), speculated at length about the location of sovereignty. To solve the circular nature of the problem and still maintain a sovereignty, Rousseau invented the concept of a supreme General Will to crown the structure. In Jacques Maritain, *Man and the State* (Chicago: The University of Chicago Press, 1951), the thought that there is no true sovereignty in the political sphere is elaborated. See pp. 49 ff.

6. In law, the directors are, of course, solely liable for the conduct of the corporation. The directors have fiduciary duties of loyalty and care, and these are owed *to the corporation itself*. An overt action that will depose or constrain corporate officers must therefore come from discontented stockholders who have succeeded in legally establishing themselves as representatives of the corporation. But this final overt action will have been generated from the publics of the corporation. The law still views corporate accountability in the simpler terms of the nineteenth century.

6. OUTSIDE AND INSIDE VIEWS

1. During the 1920s, Berle commenced writing in periodicals concerning the responsibility of corporations. In 1932 he engaged in a classic debate with the late E. M. Dodd, Jr., of the Harvard Law School, in which Berle advocated that managers are trustees primarily for their shareholders, while Dodd argued that they have a much broader trusteeship oriented to the community at large. 1932 was also the year of publication of Berle's classic, *The Modern Corporation and Private Property* (*op. cit.*) co-authored with Gardner C. Means, and still much quoted as an earlier reference on the decline of ownership. More recently, Berle's position seems to be that the managers have in fact become trustees for the entire community, so they had best make themselves accountable by learning to respond to the public consensus.

2. Adolf A. Berle, Jr., *Power Without Property* (New York: Harcourt, Brace & Company, 1959), p. 56.

3. Professor Dale puts forth similar thoughts in his book, *The Great Organizers* (New York: McGraw-Hill Book Company, Inc., 1960), Chapter 6, "To Whom is Management Accountable?"

4. Carl Kaysen, "The Social Significance of the Modern Corporation," *American Economic Review* (May 1957), p. 316.

5. Edward S. Mason, in the Introduction to *The Corporation in Modern Society, op. cit.*, p. 4.

6. David Loth, *Swope of GE* (New York: Simon & Schuster, Inc., 1958), p. 129.

7. Ben W. Lewis, "Open Season on Bigness," *Harvard Business Review* (May-June 1959), p. 108.

8. Earl Latham, "Anthropomorphic Corporations, Elites, and Monopoly Power," *American Economic Review Proceedings*, XLVII (1957), pp. 303-310. Also, "The Body Politic of the Corporation," in Edward S. Mason, *op. cit.*, p. 218.

9. Scott Buchanan, *The Corporation and the Republic*, pamphlet (New York: The Fund for the Republic, 1957), p. 27. Other plaintiffs are George Orwell, William Whyte, Jr., Robert M. Hutchins, David Riesman, and Earl Latham.

10. John Lintner, professor of finance at the Harvard Business School, has contributed substantially to the understanding of secular trends in United States corporate financing, as part of his comprehensive work in the field of profits and the functioning of the economy for the Rockefeller Foundation. Important aspects of his work are reported in Chapter 9, "The Financing of Corporations," in Edward S. Mason, *The Corporation in Modern Society, op. cit.*, p. 166. His findings confirm the statement that there has been no evidence of a general increase in reliance upon internal sources of funds in the financing of United States corporations.

11. See Simon Kuznets, *Capital in the American Economy* (Princeton: National Bureau of Economic Research, Princeton University Press, 1961), p. 243 ff.

12. See *Economic Report of the President, 1962*, Table B-65, p. 283, which shows a mild trend of increase in reliance upon internal financing during the period 1950–1961.

13. John Lintner, "Distribution of Incomes of Corporations Among Dividends, Retained Earnings, and Taxes," *American Economic Review*, 46 (May 1956), 97-113.

14. John Lintner, "Financing of Corporations," in Edward S. Mason, *op. cit.*, pp. 184–185.

15. John Lintner, "Financing of Corporations," in Edward S. Mason, *op. cit.*, p. 189.
16. J. R. Meyer and Edwin Kuh, *The Investment Decision* (Cambridge: Harvard University Press, 1957).
17. M. A. Adelman, "The Measurement of Industrial Concentration," *Review of Economics and Statistics,* Vol. XXXIII (November 1951), pp. 269-96; and "A Current Appraisal of Concentration Statistics," *J. American Statistical Association,* 53 (1958), p. 568.

7. THE SHAREHOLDER'S ROLE

1. Herbert A. Simon, "Authority," in C. M. Arensberg, *et al., Research in Industrial Human Relations* (New York: Harper & Brothers, 1957).
2. Recent yearly experience would indicate roughly that common stock issues account for no more than 5 per cent of total sources of funds for United States corporations in the aggregate.
3. Management literature in recent years reflects this controversy. There have been skeptical evaluations of the role of the owners in operating management. For example, Moses Richter, president, United Mills Corporation, writing in H. B. Maynard's *Top Management Handbook* (New York: McGraw-Hill Book Company, 1960), p. 1061, states :"Many of the vacant textile mills in the South today are vacant because stockholders, often concentrated within the controlling family, insisted on high dividends at the expense of the business' future."

Another view of ownership as a dubious steward was expressed in the Standard and Poor Corporation's publication, *The Outlook* (October 3, 1960), p. 602: "Firms with stock-owning managements may not always be a good investment—the assurance of control might make for complacency or otherwise work against objective judgment."

A further questioning look at ownership was expressed by the dean of a graduate management school: "The large family-owned corporations in India are an interesting example. Many of them are not wealth-producing organizations for the society; they are private vehicles for the speculation of the owners. They are also a place to plant the members of the family in one sinecure or another, and to take care of the retinue of faithful followers."

Also, a recent elementary study on this topic is helpful. See Ernest Dale, *The Great Organizers, op. cit.,* Appendix to Chapter 6, p. 239. Dale examines the influence of "partial proprietors" in selected corporations and demonstrates that these active part-owners can make substantial contributions to management. The study is not conclusive.

4. William Z. Ripley, *op. cit.*, Chap. IV.
5. United States Congress, House of Representatives, *Report of the Committee Appointed Pursuant to House Resolutions 429 and 504 to Investigate the Concentration of Control of Money and Credit*, 62d Congress, 2d Session, Feb. 28, 1913, p. 147.
6. Institutional investment firms, also often termed *financial intermediaries*, are a general category that includes all life and non-life insurance companies, banks, savings and loan associations, public and private pension funds, mutual investment funds, and government lending institutions. Of these, two are of particular interest in this writing (the mutual funds and the pension funds) because they are heavy investors in common stocks.
7. The authoritative picture of the financial intermediary in the United States economy is set forth in Raymond W. Goldsmith, *Financial Intermediaries in the American Economy since 1900* (Princeton: Princeton University Press, 1958).
8. Source for Table 2 and Table 3 is Board of Governors of the Federal Reserve System, *Flow of Funds/Savings Estimates*, Supplement No. 2, 1959.
9. See Peter H. Vermilye, vice-president, Morgan Guaranty Trust Co. of N. Y., "Common Stocks for Pension Funds," address delivered at the New York University Pension Trust Conference, October 6, 1960, pp. 2–4.
10. J. A. Livingston, *The American Stockholder* (Philadelphia: J. B. Lippincott & Company, 1958).
11. Adolf A. Berle, Jr., *Power without Property* (New York: Harcourt, Brace & Company, 1959), p. 54.
12. Victor L. Andrews, "Pension Funds in the Securities Markets," *Harvard Business Review* (Nov.-Dec. 1959), p. 102.
13. See Edward S. Mason, *The Corporation and Modern Society*, *op. cit.*, p. 199.

8. THE DIRECTORS

1. Cited in Don Votaw, *Legal Aspects of Business Administration* (Englewood Cliffs, N. J.: Prentice-Hall, Inc., 1956), p. 368.
2. See John Chamberlain, "Why It's Harder and Harder to Get a Good Board," *Fortune* (November 1962), pp. 112 ff.
3. W. O. Douglas, *Democracy and Finance* (New Haven: Yale University Press, 1940), p. 53.
4. Ernest Dale, *The Great Organizers, op. cit.*, p. 214.

9. MANAGEMENT: END OF THE EMPIRIC ERA

1. Abraham Flexner, *Medical Education in The United States and Canada* (New York: The Carnegie Foundation For The Advancement of Teaching, 1910), p. 52.
2. Sylvia Porter's syndicated column (New York: Hall Syndicate, *New York Post*), May 31, 1962.
3. A. H. Raskin, "Mr. Kennedy's Guidelines—Are They Drawn Too Tight?" *The Reporter* (June 21, 1962).
4. See Kerr, Clark, *et al., Industrialism and Industrial Man* (Cambridge: Harvard University Press, 1960), for a discussion of the decline of ideology and the forecast of the growth of pluralistic industrial society.
5. For a discussion of definitional items of a profession, see A. M. Carr-Saunders and P. A. Wilson, *The Professions* (Oxford: The Clarendon Press, 1933), 1926, pp. 284–318; and Carl F. Teusch, *Professional and Business Ethics*, 1926, pp. 206–210.
6. Talcott Parsons, "The Professions and the Social Structure," in *Essays in Sociological Theory, Pure and Applied* (Glencoe, Illinois: The Glencoe Press, 1949).
7. These lesser elements are derived from William J. Goode, "Encroachment, Charlatanism, and the Emerging Profession," *American Sociological Review*, Vol. 25, No. 6 (December 1960), pp. 902–903.
8. The American Management Association was organized in 1923, has ten divisions covering all aspects of management, an extensive program of annual conferences. The AMA had 8,000 members in 1950, over 32,000 in 1961; there were 1,150 meetings with over 65,000 attending in 1961. See *AMA Annual Report, 1960-61.*

   The Society for the Advancement of Management resulted from the combination of the Taylor Society and two others in the early industrial engineering work.

   The Comite International de l'Organisation, or CIOS (International Committee on Scientific Management), organized in 1924, has since held twelve international congresses for the interchange of management experience. American management participates through a United States national committee: the Council for International Progress in Management (CIPM). Since 1950, CIPM has planned and executed study programs for almost 2,000 managers from 25 countries comprising 142 different groups.

   The National Industrial Conference Board (NICB), founded in 1916, exists to conduct research in business, economics, and management, to assemble and analyze information about economic conditions and management experience in the United States and other countries, and to disseminate results thus gained by publications, conferences, and other means to business, industry, education, and the general public. In the 1950s NICB produced 175 comprehensive studies in business policy, personnel policy, and business economics. The NICB's work is supported by about 3,700 associates or sponsors (business, labor, and educational bodies).

In 1947 the Committee for Economic Development (CED) formed its Business-Education Committee, devoted to the improvement of economic thinking, chiefly by fostering intensive discussion of economic policies between managers and advisors from the academic world. The effective activities of this Committee represent a high level of professional accomplishment, and it has provided Western society with a significant body of economic research.

9. This equivalence was observed in one of the earlier analyses of the professions. See Carr-Saunders and Wilson, *op. cit.*, p. 491.

10. A good analysis of these abilities may be found in Peter F. Drucker, "The Manager and His Work," *The Practice of Management* (New York: Harper & Brothers, 1954), Chapter 27, pp. 341 ff.

11. Talcott Parsons, *op. cit.*, pp. 34 ff.

12. See Clarence B. Randall, "The Myth of the Almighty Dollar," *The Folklore of Management* (Boston: Atlantic Monthly Press, Little Brown & Co., 1961), Chapter 5.

13. Vannevar Bush, honorary chairman of the corporation, Massachusetts Institute of Technology, and chairman of the board, Merck & Co., Inc., in an address before the Manufacturing Chemists Association, Inc., November, 1960.

10. THE THIRD CULTURE

1. C. P. Snow, *The Two Cultures and the Scientific Revolution* (New York: The Cambridge University Press, 1961).

2. There is evidence that scientists and engineers tend to rebel against nonprofessional managers. See "The Scientific Mind and the Management Mind," a study by The Opinion Research Corp., Princeton, New Jersey, 1959.

3. This figure does not take into account the thousands of proprietary "colleges" of commerce and business which offer various short-term vocational courses.

4. Leonard S. Silk, *The Education of Businessmen*, p. 22. This supplementary paper from the Committee for Economic Development, 1960, is an excellent 44-page summary of the two 1959 reports.

5. Professors Gordon and Howell defined high standards for a university faculty member: He must (1) view his field as an intellectual discipline as well as a set of skills, (2) have a comprehensive and always current command of this field, (3) be a "reasonably" good teacher, (4) continually contribute to his institution's intellectual and educational planning, and (5) generate a substantial amount of significant research, especially in the improvement of business management practice. Both 1959 studies concluded that, in terms of standards of this caliber, most business school instructors are seriously deficient.

6. Leonard S. Silk, *op. cit.*, p. 11.

7. See Abba Eban, "The Eichman Trial in Retrospect," *The Reporter* (June 21, 1962), p. 16.

8. See the recent series of publications by the Department of Church and Economic Life of the National Council of Churches of Christ in the United States of America.

9. See Luther H. Hodges, *The Business Conscience* (New Jersey: Prentice-Hall, 1963), and his article "The Gray Area in Business Ethics," *AMA Management Review* (March 1963), p. 40.

10. The comments are from John Cogley, "Wanted, Theologians," in the Catholic publication, *The Commonweal* (May 22, 1959) and cited by Monsignor George Higgins in "Morals and Economic Life," a paper for the Danforth Seminar on Religion and Morality at the Harvard Graduate Business School of Industrial Administration, 1960.

11. Published in the *New York Times*, October 17, 1946, and cited by George Higgins, *ibid.*

12. The quote is from "Christian Principles and Assumptions for Economic Life," statement adopted by the General Board of the National Council of Churches of Christ in the United States of America, September 15, 1954.

13. Clarence Randall, "The Myth of Communications," *The Folklore of Management, op. cit.*, Chapter 1.

11. THE REAL PROBLEM

1. See Geoffrey Gorer, *The American People: A Study in National Character* (New York: W. W. Norton & Company, Inc., 1948), pp. 27–41.

2. In a personal interview with the author in 1961.

3. Leland H. Jenks, "Role Structure of Entrepreneurial Personality," in *Change and the Entrepreneur*, Harvard Research Center in Entrepreneurial History (Cambridge: Harvard University Press, 1949).

4. Charles E. Lindblom, in summary of comments at the 69th Annual Meeting, A.E.A., *American Economic Review*, XLVII, No. 2 (May 1957), p. 326.

5. David Riesman, *et al.*, *The Lonely Crowd* (New Haven: Yale University Press, 1950), p. 257.

6. John K. Galbraith, *American Capitalism: The Concept of Countervailing Power* (Boston: Houghton Mifflin Company, 1952).

7. Ralph E. Cordiner, *New Frontiers for Professional Managers* (New York: McGraw-Hill Book Company, Inc., 1956), p. 19.

8. See Robert M. Hutchins, "The Corporation, and Education, Ethics, and Power," in Melvin Ansen and George Bach, *Management and Corporations 1985* (New York: McGraw-Hill Book Company, Inc., 1960), pp. 183 ff.

9. James Burnham, *The Managerial Revolution* (New York: The John Day Company, Inc., 1941).

12. ACCOUNTABILITY FOR HUMAN RESOURCES

1. For recent commentary on the results of centralized planning, see Irving Kristol, "Is the Welfare State Obsolete?", *Harpers* (June 1963), pp. 39–43. A relevant analysis of dispersed decision-making may be found in John Kenneth Galbraith, "The Role of Decentralized Decision," *American Capitalism, op. cit.*, Chapter XII.

2. See Eugene V. Rostow, *Planning for Freedom* (New Haven: Yale University Press, 1959), Chapter 3, "Capitalism as a Condition of Freedom: The Major Premise," and Chapter 15, "Is Freedom Interesting Enough?". Also, Milton Friedman, "The Relation between Economic Freedom and Political Freedom," *Capitalism and Freedom*, 1962, Chapter I.

3. Medicine and law are generally considered to be professions of individual practice. Yet the common body of knowledge in each case has been built by a finely articulated group effort over a period of decades or centuries. Moreover, there have been interesting recent speculations to the effect that medicine could have developed at an equally rapid and successful pace as a group practice, wherein an organization of physicians would have established an *organizational* reputation for competency. For one such speculation, see Milton Friedman, *Capitalism and Freedom* (Chicago: The University of Chicago Press, 1962), pp. 149–160.

4. Norbert Wiener, "Progress and Entropy," *The Human Use of Human Beings* (Boston: Houghton Mifflin Co., 1950), Chapter II.

5. Originally constructed in Paul Tillich, *The Interpretation of History* (New York: Charles Scribner's Sons, 1936), pp. 118 ff. Also see Tillich, *The Protestant Era* (Chicago: The University of Chicago Press, 1948), pp. xvi, 7, 13, 18.

6. The Bhagavad-Gita, Book II, The Yoga of Knowledge.

7. A Lawrence Lowell, *Conflict of Principle* (Cambridge: Harvard University Press, 1932).

8. For a discussion of the ethic of hard work related to the logic of industrialization, see Kerr, Clark, *et al., Industrialism and Industrial Man* (Cambridge: Harvard University Press, 1960), pp. 43 ff.

9. Douglas McGregor's book, *The Human Side of Enterprise* (New York: McGraw-Hill Book Company, Inc., 1960), is an articulate plea for management to discard outworn and unreal theories, and to profit from scientific knowledge of the realities of human behavior, in the governance of industrial enterprise. Also, see the results of the 1950 conference on management's social responsibility at New York University's business school, in Chase, *et al., The Social Responsibilities of Management* (New York: School of Commerce, Accounts, and Finance, New York University, 1950). This book contains contributions from an economist, a social scientist, a corporation chairman, and a labor leader, all of whom engaged in a panel discussion before the conference.

10. In the terminology of Harold J. Ruttenberg, Pittsburgh labor relations consultant, the opposing union philosophy is called the "mutual interest" concept.

11. The survey was conducted by Mason Haire, Edwin E. Ghiselli, and Lyman W. Porter from the Institute of Industrial Relations on the Berkeley campus, University of California. It was financed by a $75,000 grant from the Ford Foundation. An advance report of the findings is contained in *Business Week* (March 2, 1963), p. 58.

12. Quoted in H. B. Maynard, *Top Management Handbook* (New York: McGraw-Hill Book Company, 1960), p. 69.

13. This particular labor position was defined by Stanley H. Ruttenberg at the 1950 conference at New York University concerning the social responsibilities of management. See Stuart Chase, *et al., The Social Responsibilities of Management, op. cit.*

14. William H. Whyte, Jr., *The Organization Man,* p. 440.

15. Kerr, Clark, *et al., op. cit.,* p. 51.

16. See William Candell, *The Psychiatric Hospital as a Small Society* (Cambridge: Harvard University Press, 1957), for an excellent analysis of the dynamics and problems of a social system with blocked mobility.

Index

171